The Institute of Biology's
Studies in Biology no. 7

Guts

The Form and Function of the Digestive System

by John Morton *D.Sc. (Lond.)*
Professor of Zoology
University of Auckland, New Zealand

Edward Arnold

First published 1967
by Edward Arnold (Publishers) Limited,
25 Hill Street,
London, W1X 8LL

Reprinted 1971
Reprinted 1973
Reprinted 1975

Boards edition ISBN: 0 7131 2090 8
Paper edition ISBN: 0 7131 2091 6

Printed offset in Great Britain by
The Camelot Press Ltd, London and Southampton

General Preface to the Series

It is no longer possible for one textbook to cover the whole field of Biology and to remain sufficiently up to date. At the same time students at school, and indeed those in their first year at universities, must be contemporary in their biological outlook and know where the most important developments are taking place.

The Biological Education Committee, set up jointly by the Royal Society and the Institute of Biology, is sponsoring, therefore, the production of a series of booklets dealing with limited biological topics in which recent progress has been most rapid and important.

A feature of the series is that the booklets indicate as clearly as possible the methods that have been employed in elucidating the problems with which they deal. There are suggestions for practical work for the student which should form a sound scientific basis for his understanding.

1967

INSTITUTE OF BIOLOGY
41 Queen's Gate
London, S.W.7.

Preface

Like engineering, but unlike physics or chemistry, biology is centrally concerned with 'design' for particular functions. When animal organization comes to be considered as static 'pattern', it loses its chief appeal, as comparative anatomy did to some extent at the beginning of this century. The study of the digestive system was one of the first departments of functional biology. Since the great Nehemiah Grew's *The Comparative Anatomy of Stomachs and Guts Begun* in 1681 zoologists have continued to be interested in the gut. The early virtuosity of inflating, varnishing and injecting gave place at the end of that century to Swammerdam's exquisite small dissection, of a quality that has never been excelled since. With the nineteenth century came the new aids of the microtome and critical staining, while we in this century have learnt to view the whole gut anew as a living structure. The first and most obtrusive of the great systems the student finds in dissecting, it is the one whose complexity is easiest to study. More than any other it reveals the animal as a working individual rather than a piece of evidence in an evolutionary pedigree. By showing the transactions going on when the animal takes part of the environment across its boundary as food, the study of the guts is linked on the one hand with ecology, and at the other extreme comes right into biochemistry.

Auckland, 1967

J.E.M.

Contents

Introduction 1

The body of a metazoan animal is in essentials a double-walled tube. The outer layer with its integument and muscle coat forms the body wall. The inner layer, also muscle-walled and lined with epithelium, is the digestive tube or gut. The two layers become continuous where the gut opens externally, at the mouth and usually—but by no means always—at the anus.

The gut is morphologically referred to as the *enteron* and is derived from the embryonic layer known as the *endoderm.* These terms both imply the interior, yet the gut is not, properly speaking, part of the animal's inside at all. The technical terms for the space inside it, the lumen, in fact means 'daylight'. Like the skin, the lining of the gut is one of the firm boundaries of the body; but it is a permeable boundary through which, unlike most skins, foodstuffs are absorbed. These must pass through the gut wall before they can strictly be said to be 'inside' or at the real disposal of the body. A few degenerate parasites such as tapeworms have altogether lost the gut and the body wall has become permeable and absorbs directly the dissolved nutriment in which it is bathed. The latest animals of all to be carefully studied, the small phylum Pogonophora, are also gutless and absorb food by their 'beard' of filamentar tentacles.

The principal function of the gut is to prepare the ingested food for assimilation. Food is changed by physical and chemical means from its original state until its constituents have been set free as smaller and simpler molecules that can pass through the epithelial membranes and into the blood system, to be at call for further metabolism. The food of animals includes everything organic and so may vary enormously in difficulty of procuring and processing. Some foods, like egg yolk and honey, present both pure and highly concentrated nutriment; some, like blood and milk and coelomic fluid, are nutritious but of inconveniently large volume. Other foods such as plankton require prolonged filtering and concentration, while still others, such as sand, mud and sawdust, are not only heavy and bulky but also very sparse in usable nutriment. Guts will naturally then vary widely in their adaptations to the nature and bulk of different foods.

The role of the first part of the alimentary canal may involve prehension and mastication by the mouth parts, or alternatively swallowing whole, followed by storage in a crop or breaking up in a gizzard. The next major stage is that of chemical preparation or enzymic digestion, which commonly begins in the stomach. Only molecules relatively small (though quite large by comparison with most inorganic substances) can be absorbed through the gut lining, and these alone can serve as building blocks in the animal's own synthetic metabolism, or as units to be burned as fuel. Protein molecules, giants of several hundred thousand molecular weight, are broken into peptone and polypeptide chains, and finally to single amino acids. Fats are simpler substances to begin with, and are hydrolysed to fatty acids and glycerol. Carbohydrates, however complex may be their polymers, such as the polysaccharides starch, pectin, dextrin and glycogen, are hydrolysed to disaccharides and finally to monosaccharides—commonly but not always glucose.

Not only are small molecules alone absorbable, but it is a fixed rule of metabolism that complex raw materials for tissue building must be broken down to the simplest components, and reassembled to the body's own pattern. Proteins of one species, even though consisting of the identical amino acids, are never directly utilizable by another; and even individuals within a species differ in the finest details of their protein constitution. Not only is the cannibal unable to use his neighbour's protein for metabolic short cuts, even the hungry dog that ate its own tail was obliged to undo its proteins and reassemble them.

General textbooks have as a rule surveyed the digestive system and its anatomy along with the other organs class by class. Yet of all the systems the gut shows the least constancy of pattern among the members of a phylum or class. It owes its distinctive form not so much to evolutionary affinity and descent, as to its special adaptations to deal with particular foods. Many animals of quite unrelated groups show convergence in the pattern and functions of the gut.

In this book we shall attempt a functional classification of guts, primarily in accordance with the types of food they handle.

The lines of division can be made quite simple.

1. Herbivores and omnivores—a large and diverse class, but the most instructive with which to begin. The gut is here most generalized with the fullest range and complement of parts. In comparison with carnivores, the food is generally bulky and may have a large unassimilable component, though it is almost always abundant and easy to obtain.

2. Deposit feeders—ingesting large instalments of the soft substratum, the food being large in bulk, diffuse and of low nutritive content.

3. Carnivores—animals living on a more concentrated and economic diet, often ingested at long intervals. The food may be of large bulk or of small, but it is frequently hard to catch, and the gut has many specializations for prehension, dismembering and swallowing.

4. Filter feeders—continuously straining microscopic food from the water by means of cilia and mucus films, or by screens of setae. There are often elaborate devices for concentrating, sorting and transporting the fine food.

5. Fluid feeders—taking liquids from plants or animals, the gut being generally provided with a piercing and sucking apparatus, and some form

of muscular pump. The rest of the tract is of simple construction, but offering ample storage space for the fluid meal.

In the following pages we shall make a necessarily brief survey of each of these five divisions. Space will not allow any wealth of detail upon such aspects as histology or enzyme biochemistry. But histology has been referred to where it sheds light upon a special function; and in spite of the great diversity of animal foods, the basic repertoire of enzymes is in fact surprisingly constant. The really interesting cases are where unusual enzymes are developed which break down substances normally intractable to digestion.

In dealing with different groups we have given rather shorter treatment of the vertebrates than is usual. In their digestive system these constitute only a single phylum, and—by the standards of invertebrate variety—rather a homogeneous one. Vertebrates differ from invertebrates in their tendency to develop sequences of different enzymes in successive parts of the gut. Many invertebrates by contrast have a few rather wide-purpose enzymes at a common site of digestion.

In all the groups studied, rather numerous examples, even within single phyla, have been given. It is hardly possible to describe a standard gut in the way one could deal with a neurone or a mitochondrion. Describing the guts of a wide diversity of animals is not profitless repetition; it is necessary in order to show the essential lesson of the gut which is in the flexibility and adaptive resource it displays in nearly every animal group.

Herbivores and Omnivores 2

2.1 The mammalian gut

Our survey may suitably begin with the digestive tract of man, an omnivore not too highly specialized with a repertoire of enzymes that copes with a wide range of not-too-difficult foodstuffs.

As in all the vertebrates, the mammalian gut has four distinct regions, the oesophagus, the stomach, and the small intestine and large intestine. It consists throughout of a strongly muscular tube, though the two muscle layers, the outer longitudinal and the inner circular, are very varyingly developed. Within the circular layer lies a bed of vascular connective tissue, the submucosa, into which project the tips of the tubular glands of the lining mucosa. A thin mucosae muscularis layer supports the glands beneath (Fig. 2–1).

Food is forced through the gut by the muscular movements of peristalsis; these are under the control of the autonomic nervous system, and are regular and continuous. Contraction of circular muscles at and behind any point distended by food forces the contents towards the anus; peristalsis proceeds by contraction on the oral side and relaxation on the anal side of any stimulated point.

Though the course of the human gut is familiar enough, we do not always realize the changing and irregular shape of the stomach, which forms a huge, distensible storage bag churning and mixing the food by its movements. It opens like a trumpet from the oesophagus into the convex region called the *cardia;* the uppermost bulge known as the *fundus* or fornix generally remains gas-filled when food is in the stomach. Big peristaltic waves pass over the stomach at the rate of three every minute and the most vigorous churning is in the pyloric region, which opens at intervals to release food to the first part of the small intestine, the duodenum.

The gastric glands, best developed in the cardiac area, are deep crypts with separate cells secreting mucus, hydrochloric acid and enzymes, chiefly pepsin which works in a medium as strongly acid as pH 2. Pepsin breaks up proteins into shorter amino acid chains, or peptones.

The food entering the small intestine forms a milky *chyme*, of not yet

Fig. 2–1 **(a–c)** The human alimentary canal: **(a)** the whole digestive tract simplified and diagrammatic; **(b)** the stomach in peristaltic contraction; **(c)** diagrammatic cross section of the intestine.
(d–g) Histology of the human gut: **(d)** gastric mucosa; **(e)** duodenal glands and villi; **(f)** mucous glands of the large intestine; **(g)** detail of the structure of the liver, showing cells of hepatic cords, with bile canaliculi draining them, and portion of the blood sinusoid system, lightly stippled, with phagocytic cells of Kupffer applied to the sinusoid walls.

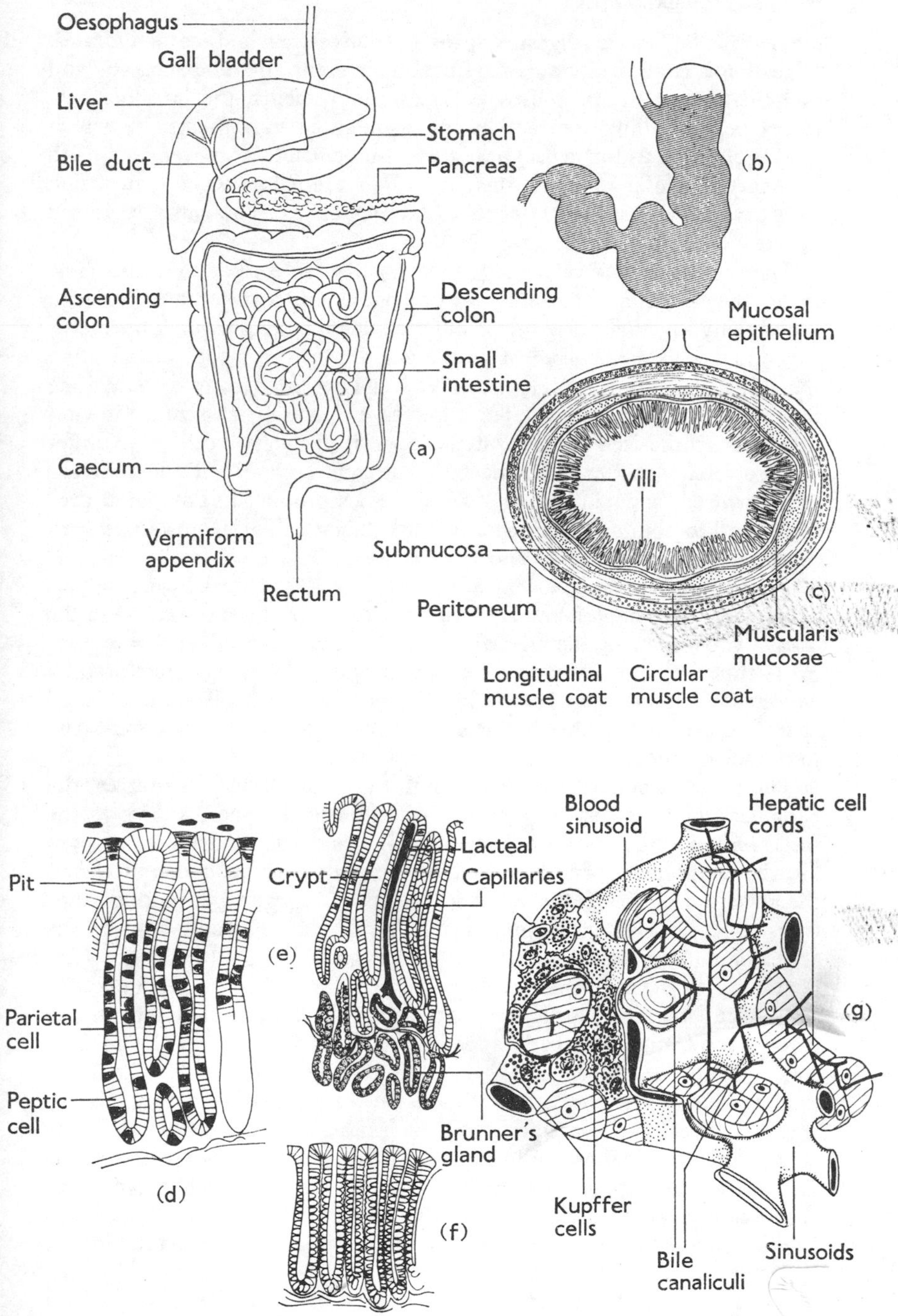

Oesophagus
Gall bladder
Liver
Stomach
Bile duct
Pancreas
(b)
Ascending colon
Descending colon
Small intestine
Mucosal epithelium
Caecum
(a)
Villi
Vermiform appendix
Submucosa
Rectum
Peritoneum
(c)
Muscularis mucosae
Longitudinal muscle coat
Circular muscle coat
Blood sinusoid
Hepatic cell cords
Lacteal
Pit
Crypt
Capillaries
(e)
(g)
Parietal cell
Peptic cell
Brunner's gland
(d)
Kupffer cells
(f)
Bile canaliculi
Sinusoids

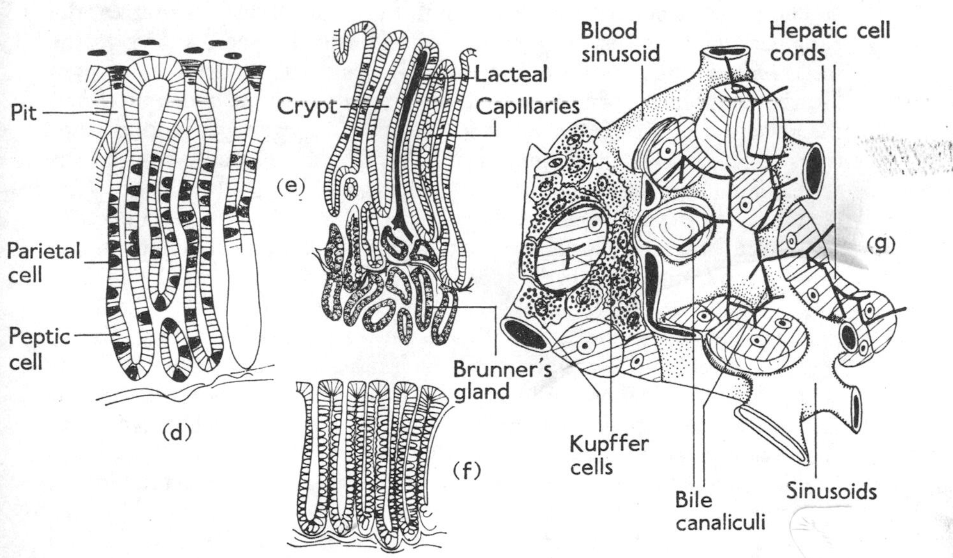

emulsified fat, partly-digested protein derivatives and carbohydrates. Digestion is continued, now in an alkaline medium, by the pancreatic and intestinal enzymes. As well as peristaltic movements, the intestine performs non-travelling contractions or segmenting movements, by which food is churned and mixed. There may also be pendular movements, with the shortening of a section of the gut by longitudinal muscular contraction so as to throw chyme from one end to another, as J. Z. Young has expressed it, like a cocktail shaker.

The pancreatic and bile ducts open together into the duodenum. The bile is the secretion of the liver, an organ unique to vertebrates. Though it has many functions, enzyme production is not among them. The liver is concerned with metabolism of amino acids from the blood, deaminating them and converting —NH_2 into urea. The liver also stores carbohydrate from the blood as glycogen, fat is stored as such and metabolized, and vitamin A is synthesized from carotene. Special phagocytic cells of Kupffer remove foreign matter from the blood stream. In addition, old red cells are destroyed, and—in the young—new ones produced. The blood proteins prothrombin and fibrinogen are synthesized. Toxic substances such as alcohol are broken down and rendered harmless.

The bile is alkaline, containing as well as bile salts the breakdown products of haemoglobin, cholesterol and lecithin. Its main digestive action is the emulsifying of fats by the bile salts, reducing their surface tension so as to break them up into a suspension of fine droplets. Bile is manufactured by columns of hepatic cells, bathed by sinusoids, or the small ultimate blood spaces, and enclosing fine channels or bile canaliculi which lead eventually to the major ducts.

The enzymes active in the small intestine come from two sources, the pancreatic juice and the secretion of the intestinal glands, known as the *succus entericus*. As well as enzymes, the pancreas contributes sodium bicarbonate which reduces the acidity of the intestinal medium. From the pancreas originate the enzyme precursors trypsinogen and chymotrypsinogen, converted to the enzymes trypsin and chymotrypsin by the activator enterokinase from the intestinal glands. This breaks up polypeptides into shorter amino acid chains, which are then broken into two-amino-acid fragments, called dipeptides, by the enzymes aminopeptidase from the intestine and carboxypeptidase from the pancreas. The final action of intestinal dipeptidase sets free the single amino acids. The intestinal and pancreatic amylase continues the work briefly begun by salivary amylase, breaking down starch and some other polysaccharides to disaccharides such as maltose and sucrose. Further intestinal enzymes such as maltase, sucrase and lactase, break down the respective disaccharides to absorbable monosaccharides, chiefly glucose and fructose.

The enzyme lipase, present both in the pancreatic and intestinal juices, hydrolyses fats to glycerol and fatty acids.

Table 1 shows the digestive enzymes with their sources of origin and

Table 1

Eaten	*Mouth* (pH 7)	*Stomach* (pH 2)	*Small intestine* (pH 7)	*Absorbed*
PROTEINS		*pepsin*; *rennin** → POLYPEPTIDES	*trypsin* (pancreas); *chymotrypsin* (pancreas) → DIPEPTIDES; *carboxypeptidase* (pancreas); *aminopeptidase* (intestine); *dipeptidase*	AMINO ACIDS
POLYSACCHARIDES	*amylase*		*amylase* (pancreas: intestine	MONOSACCHARIDES
DISACCHARIDES			*maltase*; *sucrase*; *lactase* (intestine)	MONOSACCHARIDES
FATS			*lipase* (pancreas: intestine); *bile salts* (liver)	COLLOIDAL FATS
		FATTY ACIDS GLYCERINE		FATTY ACIDS GLYCERINE

* Coagulates milk proteins in early life.

their sequential action, with later ones acting upon the progressively simpler products of earlier splittings. The series present in the human gut, though lacking the enzymes necessary for many of the more difficult jobs, is very representative of the digestive competence of higher animals.

Intestinal digestion leaves a finely divided milky suspension known as *chyle*, whose contents are now ready to be absorbed. The efficiency of uptake by the gut wall varies greatly from region to region. Some drugs, such as morphine, are absorbed even within the mouth. Through the gastric mucosa may pass simple compounds such as salts, glucose and especially alcohol. Thus is seen the appropriateness of the oil-dressed hors d'oeuvre, which derives from the spoonful of olive oil with which the Romans were said to begin a banquet, to coat the gastric mucosa with a film delaying the absorption of alcohol. But by far the most active absorption of all is from the upper part of the small intestine, through the extensive surfaces of the villi, minute, tag-like processes in continual movement, contracting and expanding while bathed with the digested food. Both monosaccharides and amino acids pass by active transport against the diffusion gradient through the epithelium into the blood plexus inside the villus, to be conducted to the portal circulation. Glucose transport is facilitated by conversion into a phosphate sugar complex in the absorptive cells. Fats may be taken up by alternative routes: either after complete hydrolysis by way of the portal circulation, or—more generally—as a fine suspension of whole fat droplets, which passes into the lacteals, little channels in each villus, leading ultimately to the thoracic duct of the lymphatic system.

The large intestine is a wide tube with no digestive powers, its epithelium being characterized by its abundance of mucus glands. The contents of the gut remaining after digestion and absorption are here further concentrated by the large uptake of water. After some 36 hours, solid or semi-solid faeces are produced. With a normal diet, very little of the faeces are comprised of undigested or indigestible food. Faeces continue indeed to be formed during starvation, and contain chiefly the residues of bile and other internal secretions, leucocytes, sloughed-off cells of the epithelium, and vast numbers of bacteria, both living and dead. The colour of the faeces is due to the presence of stercobilin, and other pigments of haemoglobin breakdown from the bile; their evil odour comes largely from the compounds indole and skatole, as well as hydrogen sulphide, derived from the bacterial breakdown of certain amino acids. Carbohydrates are also bacterially fermented with the production of carbon dioxide and methane.

The most vital role of the large intestine is probably, however, the work of its bacterial flora, the process of vitamin synthesis. The colon bacteria invade the infant of a few days' old and remain important to it throughout life. Animals are able to manufacture few if any vitamins for themselves, and for our whole bodily production of the vitamin B complex (riboflavine, nicotinic acid, vitamin B_{12} and vitamin K) we are dependent on the synthetic work of these microscopic symbionts. Thus, after the administration of many oral antibiotics an alternative supplement to the body's vitamin supply is temporarily necessary.

2.2 Cellulose digestion in rodents and ungulates

The most interesting special adaptations of the mammalian gut are found among those groups—chiefly rodents and ungulates—ingesting a massive diet of plant food with much cellulose. Here the stomach, colon and caecum are enlarged as storage and fermentation chambers, and harbour an especially important microflora of bacterial anaerobes or facultative anaerobes. Such symbionts occur in the most capacious parts of the gut where food remains longest; they are found in the colon where bacterial digestion occurs in huge proportions, not only in ruminants, but such other herbivores as the horse and the rabbit. Bacteria are also abundant in the stomach of ruminants (cattle, sheep, antelope and deer), where they meet with the food before the contact of digestive enzymes. In the ruminant stomach also live special populations of ciliate Protozoa.

The activity of the gut bacteria seems undoubtedly to offer extra opportunities for the digestion of 'difficult' carbohydrates such as cellulose, which are converted in the stomach and elsewhere to volatile and absorbable fatty acids. Acetic acid can be formed *in vitro* by inoculating a suspension of cotton-wood cellulose with rumen contents if kept at body temperature. From various complex carbohydrates, formic, acetic, propionic, butyric, succinic and lactic acids may be produced in the rumen and—contrary to traditional belief—absorbed there. Blood from the rumen contains these acids in high ratio, and in the sheep they account for about one quarter of the carbon assimilated from all carbohydrate sources. Carbon dioxide and methane are also produced by fermentation, being either eructed or passed by the lungs. The watery milieu and optimum pH in the bacterial chamber are maintained by copious saliva, rich in bicarbonate.

We have seen already the importance of gut bacteria in the synthesis of vitamin B. In the ruminant stomach they must also be of value in providing food for the special microfauna of ciliates, which are ultimately digested to provide additional protein to the host. It would appear, too, that the gut bacteria can utilize non-protein nitrogen for the ultimate provision of protein.

The ciliate Protozoa of the rumen appear to play no part in cellulose decomposition, though they digest starch, grains of which can be identified in various stages of assimilation in their cells. These ciliates belong to the order Entodiniomorpha; two examples are illustrated, *Entodinium caudatum* with a circlet of oral cilia and three posterior processes, the largest of which is said to serve as a rudder, and *Epidinium ecaudatum* with two tufts of still cirri at the oral end, and a so-called 'ventral skeletal plate' which is an important store of polysaccharide. As well as starch grains, they ingest protein-forming and cellulose-digesting micro-organisms by the small cytostome.

The ruminant stomach is illustrated from the cow in Fig. 2–2. The true stomach or abomasum, which is alone provided with peptic glands and opens straight to the pylorus is, in the calf, much larger than all the rest. Here it provides the milk-coagulating enzyme known as rennin, and is hence known as the 'rennet stomach'. The remaining three chambers are

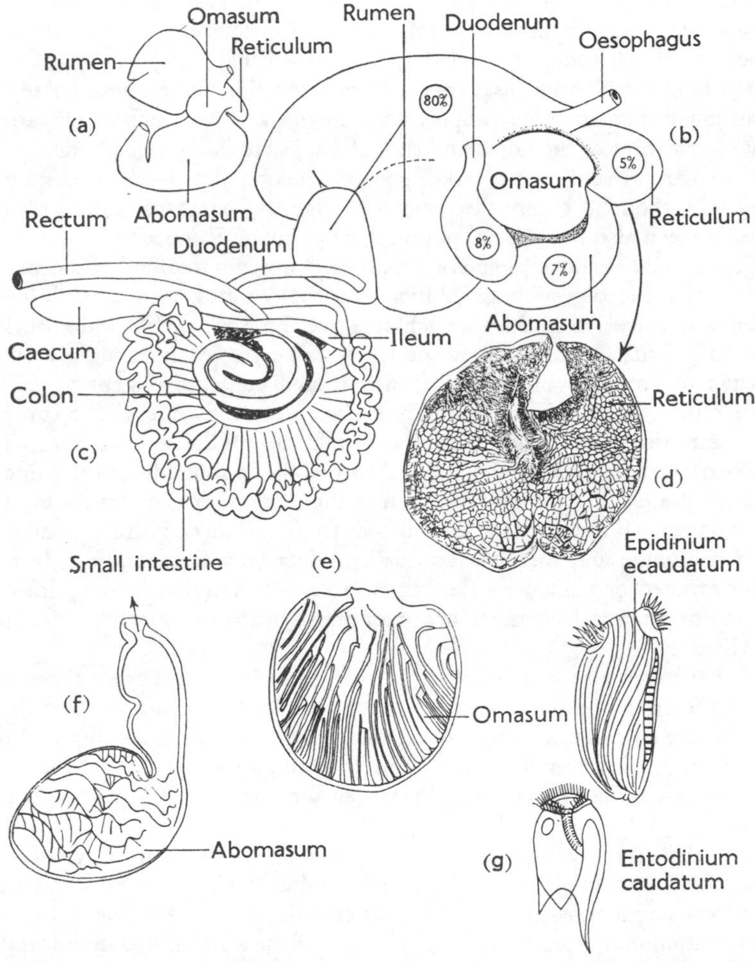

Fig. 2–2 The ruminant stomach and its ciliates: **(a)** stomach of newly born calf; **(b)** stomach; **(c)** intestinal tract of adult ox; **(d–f)** interior of reticulum, omasum and abomasum; **(g)** *Epidinium* and *Entodinium*.

the rumen or paunch, the reticulum or honeycomb (its lining is the source of honeycomb tripe) and the omasum, variously called the manifold, maniplies or psalterium, from the page-like appearance of the thin folds of epithelium reaching across its lumen. These three chambers have a horny stratified lining epithelium, and are really to be looked on as oesophageal sacculations. Small at birth, the rumen finally comes to account for 80 per cent of the total stomach capacity. In the feeding ruminant grass passes from the oesophagus into the reticulum. Here it is made up into small compacted balls of cud, and in this fashion returned to the mouth, where it is chewed over at more leisure. On re-swallowing, the food returns to the rumen, where it is subjected to bacterial digestion and to the action of ciliates. The remaining contents then pass between the straining leaves of the omasum, and onwards to the abomasum, or true stomach, and so to the pylorus.

The hares and rabbits (Lagomorpha) take in a bulky diet of grass and greenstuffs. The stomach is large and simple, but there is a long caecum with a well-developed vermiform appendix with populations of iodophile bacteria digesting cellulose, as well as the bacteria producing vitamin B. Hares and rabbits do not ruminate but re-ingest the faecal pellets, giving the food a second passage through the digestive system and allowing micro-organisms to act twice upon it. There are no stomach ciliates, as in ruminants, and no gastric uptake of volatile acids.

2.3 Birds

The diet of birds is as widely varied as that of mammals. The herbivores include seed-eaters, fruit-eaters, pollen and nectar-feeders, grazers, leaf-eaters and root-eaters. Among the carnivores we shall find predators on fish, aquatic invertebrates, insects and land vertebrates, as well as carrion-eaters.

The tempo of life in birds is invariably swift and alert. Food is speedily swallowed with no interval for mastication. The margins of the jaws are covered with horny investments forming the beak, and only in seed-crackers and flesh-tearers does the beak assist in the first phase of comminution of the food.

The small salivary glands primarily produce mucoid lubricants, not enzymes, and the food passes quickly by peristalsis to the crop. In the swift family, especially in the S.E. Asian *Collocalia*, the salivary glands secrete an adhesive material used in the construction of the nest.

A bird's crop forms a spacious diverticulum of the oesophagus, muscular-walled but thin and distensible. In the pigeon and fowl it is suspected that it secretes an amylase, and it is known in breeding pigeons to produce a nutritive 'milk', rich in fat and protein, but having no sugar.

The stomach is divided into an anterior glandular part or proventriculus, followed by a muscular chamber or gizzard, an organ well known and much studied in birds. In fish-eaters such as the heron (Fig. 2–3b), the proventriculus may be very distensible and act as a food store. But its chief role is the secretion of gastric juices with peptic enzymes, and the initiation of the main digestion. In carnivores the gizzard may serve chiefly as a storage place in which proteolytic digestion gets under way. In graminivorous birds the gizzard reaches by far its best development, and its strong circular muscle coat is differentiated into bilaterally symmetrical, semi-autonomous masses (Fig. 2–3a). Vigorous rhythmic contractions are responsible for the grinding and triturating of hard food, and hard surfaces

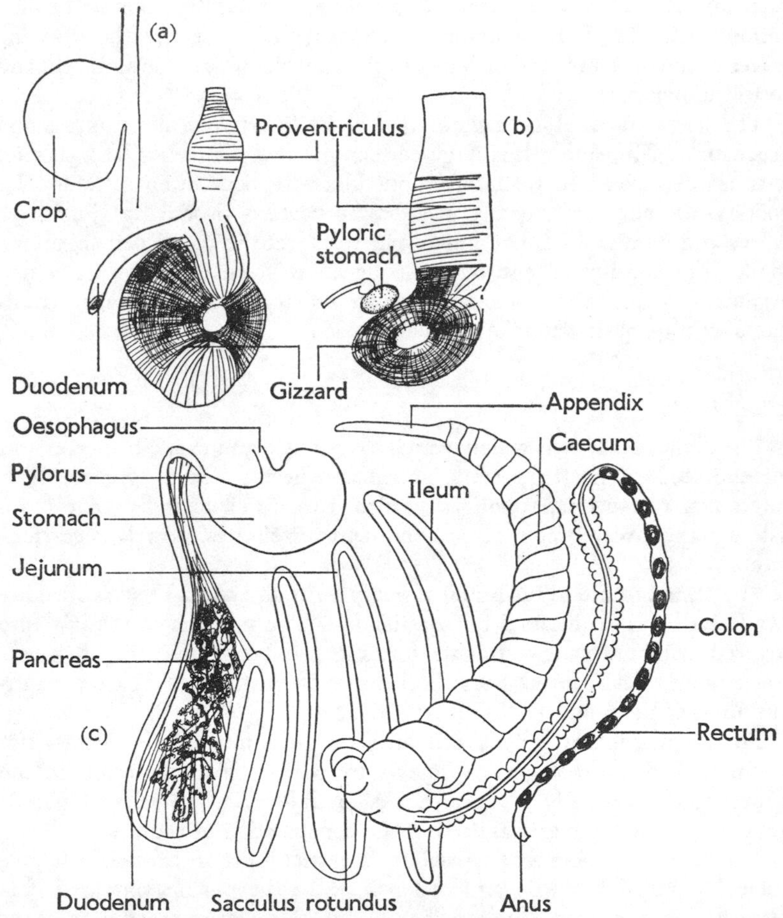

Fig. 2–3 (**a**) Crop and stomach of the peacock, *Pavo*. (**b**) Stomach (with proventriculus, gizzard and pyloric stomach) of the heron, *Ardea cinerea*. (**c**) Alimentary canal of the rabbit, *Oryctolagus canaculus*.

are provided also by the grit and small gizzard stones regularly ingested by many species. The lining of the gizzard secreted by special tubular glands is composed of a greenish brown, horny proteinaceous substance called *koilin*. In herons and some other aquatic feeding birds there is also a tiny post-pyloric stomach, and from the long hair-like processes sometimes found in this, as in the darters, it appears to act as a filter.

Many birds, in particular the herbivorous and graminivorous Galliformes, have two long intestinal caeca, with thickened lymphoidal walls. It has been suggested that these are the seat of microbial digestion of cellulose. It is known, too, that the honey guide, *Indicator minor*, can subsist for long periods on a diet of pure beeswax, which is broken down to usable compounds by the intestinal microflora.

2.4 Land vertebrates in general

The amphibians and reptiles have for the most part a very unspecialized gut, with a short wide gullet, a simple stomach, and teeth and jaws used simply for prehension and swallowing. From the reptilian level, the birds and the mammals have become specialized in very different ways. With diversity of diet, the birds have lost the teeth and replaced them with the horny sheath of the bill. But in the mammals, the dentition has become as widely diversified as the diet. In grazing rodents and ungulates, the teeth may develop continuous pulps and high enamel crowns. The carnivores have acquired a sharp dentition with shearing and cutting surfaces. With extreme microphagous diet, as in the various groups of anteaters, the teeth are reduced or lost and the tongue hypertrophied. In the baleen whales horny filters replace the true dentition. The most general achievement of the mammals is, however, their ability to masticate bulky food into small pieces; their jaw muscles and bones are uniquely simplified and strengthened, while—as also in birds—a respiratory passage has been established independent of the food channel.

2.5 The insect gut

The insects are small, persistent and prolific land arthropods. As well as to flying power and specialized life histories, they owe much of their success to highly specific adaptation to numerous apparently unpromising diets. Enzymes have been acquired, in various adults and larvae, for dealing with substances including cellulose, pollen, wood, wax, silk, keratin and collagen. On the other hand, a generalized insect such as the cockroach and some other Orthoptera may have a range of diet not greatly different from that of man, and it is with the gut of such an insect omnivore that we must first be concerned.

The alimentary canal of every insect consists of a fore-gut, mid-gut and hind-gut (Fig. 2–4a–d). The first and third are derived from the ectodermal

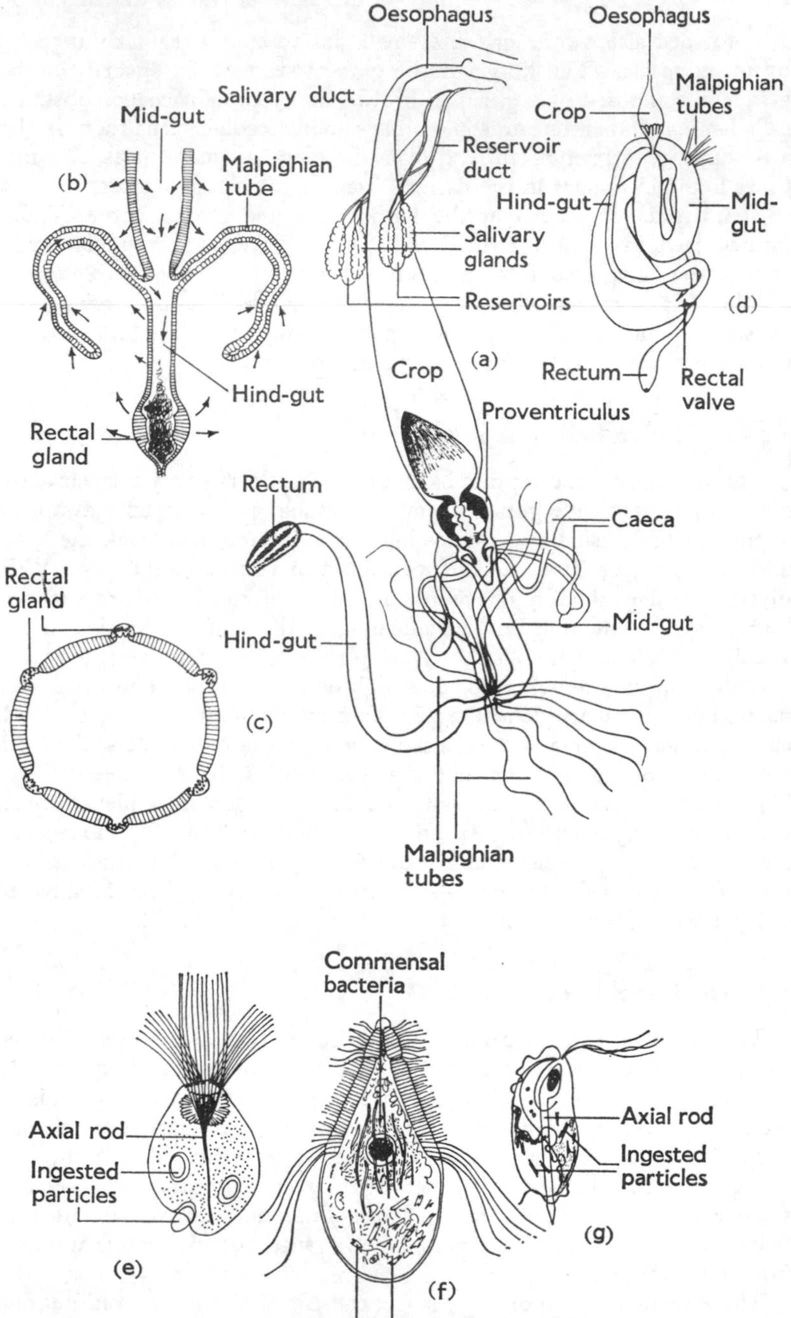

Mid-gut
(b)
Malpighian tube
Hind-gut
Rectal gland
Rectal gland
(c)
Oesophagus
Salivary duct
Reservoir duct
Salivary glands
Reservoirs
(a)
Crop
Proventriculus
Rectum
Caeca
Hind-gut
Mid-gut
Malpighian tubes
Oesophagus
Malpighian tubes
Crop
Hind-gut
Mid-gut
(d)
Rectum
Rectal valve
Commensal bacteria
Axial rod
Ingested particles
(e)
(f)
Wood fragments
Axial rod
Ingested particles
(g)

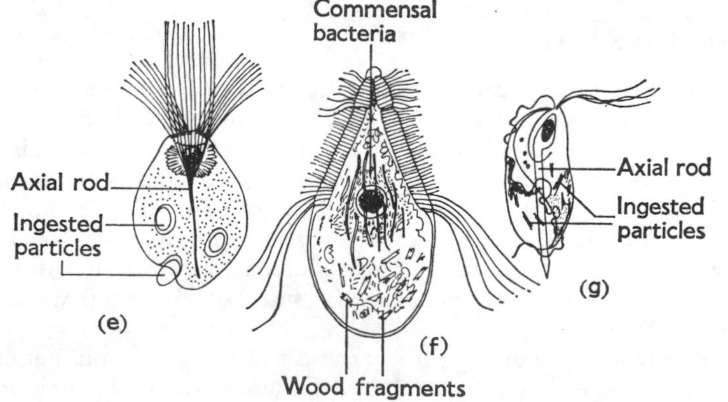

stomodaeum and proctodaeum respectively, and as such are lined with a thin extension of the cuticle that covers the outer surfaces of the body. The mid-gut, or mesenteron, generally regarded as forming the true stomach, originates from the embryonic endoderm. As in all the arthropods, cilia and mucous cells are unknown, and food is impelled through the gut by muscular peristalsis.

The cockroach has very generalized mouth parts with strong mandibles for biting and tearing, and the muscles of the pharynx are adapted for swallowing coarse particles. Into the pharynx open by long ducts two pairs of salivary glands, anterior and posterior, associated with two thin-walled vesicles also with long ducts. As well as moistening the food and lubricating the mouth parts the saliva contains a powerful amylase and invertase, initiating the digestion of starch and disaccharides.

The narrow oesophagus widens into a long fusiform crop which—as well as a spacious chamber—is an important seat of digestion. As well as the saliva mixed with the food, the enzymes carried forward from the mid-gut are also active here. Little if anything is absorbed in the crop, which is practically impermeable to water. Sugar will not pass its lining, but olive oil will, as may be discovered by studies of absorption with a ligated crop. The general lining of the fore-gut is of cuticle which is massively thickened in the proventriculus, or gizzard, a spherical chamber lying immediately behind the crop. This structure shows every development in insects from a mere muscular sphincter to a powerful triturating chamber, endowed as in the cockroach with strong circular muscles and six strong radially inserted teeth. Behind the teeth, a corresponding row of hairy cushions serves as a food strainer. Crushed contents from the gizzard are returned to the crop to further digestion while the fluid products finally seep through the filter to the mid-gut.

In the mesenteron the epithelium bears no lining cuticle as such but in almost all insects is kept free from abrasion by the gut contents by a delicate detached sheath of chitin and protein combined, known as the peritrophic membrane, which replaces the protection afforded by the mucous lining of the vertebrate gut. The peritrophic membrane is very permeable to molecules, keeping back only dyes of large molecular weight and allowing enzymes and the products of digestion to pass without hindrance. In the cockroach the peritrophic membrane is produced directly by the under-

Fig. 2–4 **(a–d)** The insect gut: **(a)** alimentary canal of the cockroach, *Periplaneta americana*, dissected to show the interior of the proventriculus; **(b)** diagram of the water circulation in the insect gut and excretory system; **(c)** section of the rectum showing the arrangement of the rectal glands in Orthoptera and Coleoptera; **(d)** gut of the termite, *Eutermes*, showing the rectal pouch. (After various authors.)
(e–g) Gut flagellates: **(e)** *Lophomonas blattarum* (20 μ) from the cockroach; **(f)** *Trichonympha collaris* (250 μ); **(g)** *Trichomonas termopsidis* (30 μ) from *Zootermopsis*.

lying cells in thin concentric sheets, the inner layers being periodically passed backwards as investments of the faeces.

The fore-gut lining projects into the mid-gut, directing the contents into the cylinder formed by the peritrophic membrane. The surface of the mid-gut is increased by the outgrowth of five or six long blunt-tipped caeca near its anterior end, and the peritrophic membrane simply spans the mouth of these. Secretion and absorption within the mid-gut and its caeca are generally carried out by the same cells, which in the cockroach undergo alternate phases of activity. The cells may also store absorbed or metabolized substances, such as fat droplets after a sugar meal. Numerous enzymes are contributed by the mid-gut cells including protease, lipase and maltase. With the acid crop contents, the salivary amylase works best at a pH of 5·9, and the mid-gut proteases at 7·5, though they may function efficiently well over to the acid side of neutrality. The so-called 'protease' has several components, a trypsin (though never a pepsin) acting on whole proteins and peptidases splitting the later products, including amino-polypeptidase active at the NH^2 linkage, a carboxypolypeptidase attacking —COOH groups and dipeptidase hydrolysing all dipeptides. While the proteinases are active in the lumen the peptidases seem to be concentrated within the cells.

At the boundary of the mid-gut with the hind-gut a series of threadlike excretory organs, the Malpighian tubules, discharge their contents into the lumen. Insinuating their way through the whole visceral mass and among the lobules of the fat body, these organs are finer and more numerous in the Orthoptera than in most other insects. Their chief product is uric acid.

The hind-gut, like the fore-gut, has a thin lining cuticle, but it is readily permeable to water. It begins with a longer and narrower colon, opening into a short, wide rectum, where the lining cells tend to separate into six pads or folds known as rectal glands. In the Orthoptera the faeces become progressively drier as they pass back and the rectal glands play a large part in the absorption of water. Dry faecal pellets are produced after 9–13 hours. They are invested with peritrophic membrane which is drawn backwards by spinules on the hind-gut cuticle.

Certain species of cockroach, and also the termites (Isoptera), rely heavily upon a diet of wood; and just as in herbivorous mammals the digestion of cellulose is largely the role of symbiotic micro-organisms. Bacteria probably play a smaller role in wood-feeding insects than do the flagellate Protozoa. In the wood-feeding cockroach, *Cryptocercus*, and even more importantly in the termites (with the exception of the 'highest' family, the Termitidae), the hind-gut is enlarged to form a pouch of greater capacity than all the rest of the gut together. This chamber contains a teemingly rich population of large and complex flagellates belonging to the order Hypermastigina; they are frequently to be found packed closely in a seemingly pure mass. Fig. 2–4e–g illustrates the characteristic shapes in some of their genera. *Lophomonas* is typical of the common cockroach and *Trichomonas* and the very large *Trichonympha* inhabit the termite gut. The gut flagellates can be clearly seen to ingest fine particles of wood into their cytoplasm, different species perhaps playing different roles in digesting the various constituents of wood. It has been suggested, too, that the flagellates contain symbiotic populations of bacteria that do the actual digesting. Termites can live on a pure cellulose diet so long as they are not deprived of their flagellates by starvation, or exposure to high temperatures or high oxygen tensions. In *Zootermopsis*, some two-thirds of the material absorbed from wood has been rendered assimilable by flagellates.

A wide variety of carbohydrates contribute to the composition of wood, of which the first, lignin (some 18–38 per cent of the total), is—so far as we know—never digested. Cellulose (40–62 per cent of the total) is, however, not infrequently broken down to assimilable sugars. In wood-eating insects where gut Protozoa are not active, cellulose-digesting bacteria are frequently to be found. Extensive bacterial digestion within the gut is less feasible than in the mammals for the passage of the food is too fast, but the many cellulose-splitting bacteria present in rotting wood may continue their work after ingestion. Some lamellicorn beetle larvae that bore in wood have fermentation chambers forming enlargements of the hind-gut in which bacterial action is fostered. A wood-eating cockroach *Panesthia* keeps cellulose-decomposing bacteria in the crop.

It has been claimed that some insects, such as certain wood-boring beetles, produce true cellulolytic enzymes, while others—and probably most wood-feeding insects—are unable to digest cellulose and depend very greatly on the starch and sugar content of the wood.

Many insects digest 'difficult' foods with high efficiency. Resistant animal proteins, such as the fibrous collagen of tendons, are digested by blow-fly larvae. The clothes moth, *Tineola*, breaks down silk as well as the keratin of hair and feathers. A strong reducing agent first operates in opening the stable S—S linkages binding the folded polypeptide chains. *Galleria* larvae, which feed on honeycombs, are able to utilize the high molecular weight esters and fatty acids of beeswax.

2.6 The molluscan gut

The Mollusca are a huge and diverse phylum, ranging from slugs to cuttle-fish, and they are equally varied in their diet. They show a basic unity of plan to which adaptations have been richly and endlessly applied; even such a plastic system as the gut keeps a strong homology throughout the whole group.

The most primitive molluscs we know today, such as chitons and early gastropods, are herbivores or omnivores, rasping their food from a hard substratum, or sweeping up fine organic particles from the surface. Molluscs were not primitively biters or browsers so much as scrapers and rakers; and the limpets and topshells typify this habit today among the Gastropoda. A most characteristic organ, unique to the Mollusca, is the radula, the tooth-bearing ribbon borne within the buccal mass upon the odontophore or tongue. In all grazing molluscs, as the snout is held close to the ground, the tongue is rolled forward so that the radula upon its free surface is expanded and drawn across the dilated mouth opening. The fine teeth engage the substratum, abrading and dislodging, and the material so gathered is then swept back into the buccal mass as the mouth momentarily closes. On retraction, the particles on the radula are transferred in conveyor belt fashion to the ciliated lining of the roof of the buccal mass, and back into the oesophagus.

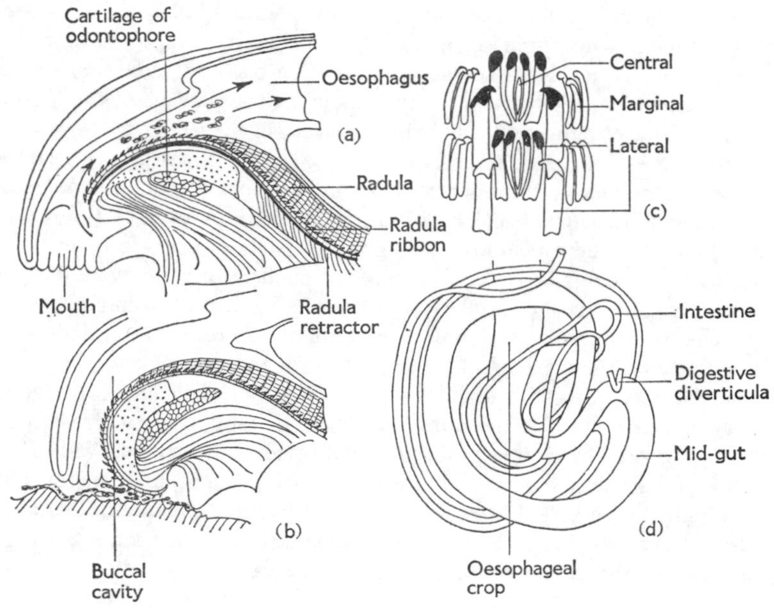

Fig. 2–5 (**a & b**) Diagrammatic sagittal sections of the buccal mass of a prosobranch gastropod, showing the action of the radula. (**c**) Two rows of radular teeth of the limpet, *Patella vulgata*. (**d**) Alimentary canal of the limpet *Patella vulgata*, omitting the buccal mass. (After FRETTER and GRAHAM.)

Seen in longitudinal section in Fig. 2–5a and b, the odontophore carries the chitinous ribbon of the radula, studded with microscopic teeth, in a V-shaped depression on its upper surface. This can be opened widely when the odontophore is protracted and partly closed at the retractor stroke. The odontophore is sometimes likened to a pulley over which the ribbon slides, but the whole radula is in fact fixed at any one time and its movement is effected by the rolling of the whole tongue. Only a few rows of teeth are brought to bear at one time, and these finally become worn and detached, as the ribbon shifts slowly forwards round the edge of the tongue.

The limpets (Patellacea) are herbivorous gastropods adapted for grazing on the barest and seemingly most unproductive of hard substrates. The food of *Patella vulgata* consists of tiny filamental algae, wave-lodged diatoms and debris, and minute algae sporelings which are grazed soon after settlement. The radular teeth are strong and robust (Fig. 2–5c) and must be rapidly renewed; the functional part of the radula is being constantly replaced from the long caecum, which is several times the length of the body and thrown into half a dozen or more coils.

The limpet gut is well designed for handling bulky food. The oesophagus forms a wide tube running back from the buccal mass to serve as a storage chamber. Turning forward, it becomes continuous with the stomach, which passes insensibly into the first part of the intestine. This whole section of the gut forms the site of digestion which begins with the extracellular action of enzymes derived from three sources. Small salivary glands and paired oesophageal pouches produce amylase; from the openings of the digestive diverticula a wide range of enzymes is mixed with the food, including protease, amylase and lipase. In the limpet, as in many other herbivorous molluscs, small but significant traces of cellulase have recently been found.*

In the limpet, the intestine is long and narrow thrown into six or more complete loops embedded in the digestive gland. Bulky faeces are continuously produced and elaborated into a firm rope by weak peristalsis, being discharged into the mantle cavity above the head.

In all molluscs the digestive diverticula form a large brown gland, built up of innumerable small follicles from the ramifying ducts. The lining cells play several roles. They absorb the products of extracellular digestion, not only in soluble form but also as finely divided particles which undergo further intracellular digestion. They produce enzymes which are both active within the cells and are also secreted into the stomach, often by the rounding off and detachment of the whole cell or its tip. By this means, too, waste material is extruded into the stomach, including particles finally indigestible, and dark spherules of plant pigments and other coloured wastes extracted from the blood. Finally, the digestive gland acts as a lime store, maintaining in certain cells a reserve of calcium salts for shell-building and finely regulating the pH of the gut contents.

In contrast with the limpet, the sea-hare—*Aplysia*—is a browsing herbivore, cropping succulent red, green and brown algae. The alimentary tract (Fig. 2–6b) is well adapted to deal with this fodder. The anterior part is

* The crop of *Helix*, the land-snail, is a prolific store of enzymes, much resorted to by the biochemist. Cellulose digestion is highly efficient in *Helix* and is claimed to be the work of bacterial populations which flourish in both the crop and the intestine.

much enlarged into a thin-walled and distensible crop, followed by two gizzards. The first is lined by heavy chitinous teeth, closely meshing to form a mincer which triturates the food. Coarser particles of weed are intercepted by the slender flexible teeth of the second gizzard which serves as a filter. Through this whole space the enzymes from the digestive gland are well circulated as food is shunted back and forth through stomach, gizzard and crop. After extracellular digestion food is forced by pressure of the stomach wall into the digestive diverticula, where absorption and

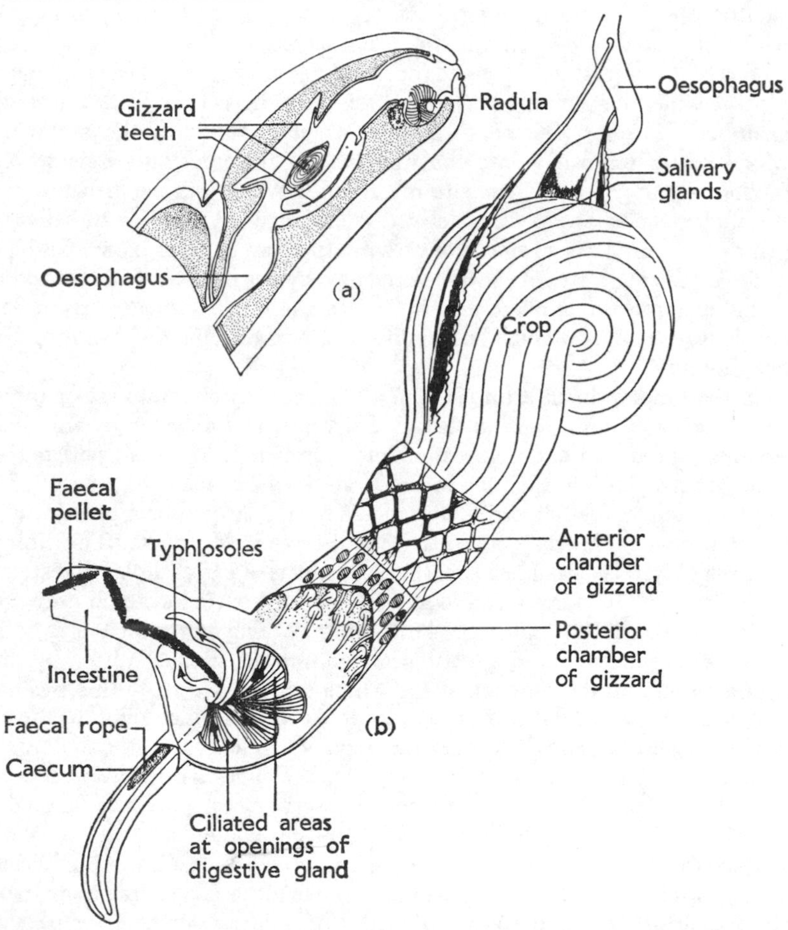

Fig. 2–6 Some gastropod digestive systems: (**a**) sagittal section of the head shield of *Philine aperta*, showing the buccal mass and the toothed oesophageal gizzard; (**b**) alimentary canal of the sea hare, *Aplysia punctata*, omitting the buccal mass and the intestine. (Based on FRETTER (**a**) and HOWELLS (**b**).)

final intracellular digestion begins. The indigestible residues pass into a narrow caecum of the stomach, in which firm rods of faeces are elaborated by mucous secretion and ciliary action.

2.7 Echinodermata: sea urchin

In most of their structure and functions, the echinoderms only remotely resemble other Metazoa; they clearly form an evolutionary branch following their own principles of design. We shall deal here with the regular sea-urchins, *Echinus* and their relatives, which can best be described as unselective omnivores. They crop growing algae and scrape off encrusting

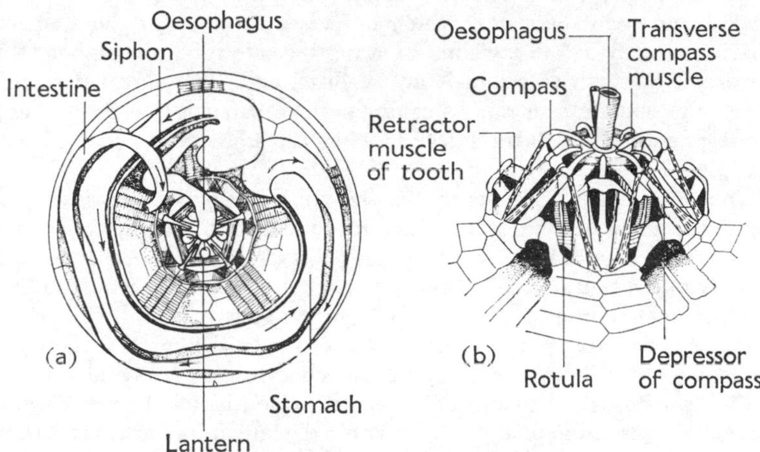

Fig. 2–7 The gut of the sea-urchin, *Echinus esculentus:* **(a)** the whole alimentary canal in situ after removal of the upper hemisphere of the shell; **(b)** details of the Aristotle's lantern and its musculature.

organisms such as polyzoa, hydroids and barnacles; much sand, small stones and indigestible debris may also be taken in. Like limpets, sea-urchins appear to occupy a definite resting place, often a scar or depression hollowed out by abrasion with the spines. By means of the hydrostatic tube-feet and stilt-like use of the spines, they make wide grazing forays in the surrounding neighbourhood.

The sea-urchins are equipped with an unique abrading organ as remarkable as the molluscan radula, in the complex of five strong jaws surrounding the mouth and oesophagus and known as Aristotle's lantern (Fig. 2–7). Each jaw forms heavily calcified plate, investing a chisel-like tooth, five of which converge to protrude at their tips through the opened mouth. Aborally, at the roof of the lantern, the jaws are linked by alternating pieces known as *rotulae*. Overlying the rotulae are five radially disposed pieces referred to as the compasses. The radially set jaw-retractor muscles, by asymmetrical contractions, can poise or pivot the whole lantern tip in one or another direction from the mouth. Other muscles are responsible for the co-ordinated opening and closing of the teeth, and for lowering and raising the roof of the lantern to circulate respiratory water in the coelomic space surrounding it.

The tube feet of the urchin may act as the first collectors of food, passing material to the mouth to be seized by the rhythmically opening and closing jaws. These may also engage like a mechanical grab on the substratum below and seize food directly. The lantern jaws are then raised to bring their load into contact with the lips of the pharynx, where a lubricatory mucus is also supplied to the lantern. Food is passed upwards by vigorous peristalsis through the muscular oesophagus. There is also a pronounced inward movement of water, which by-passes the loop of the stomach, arriving directly at the intestine by a narrow side tube, the siphon, that leaves the stomach to rejoin it at the distal end. The siphonal current appears to operate as a rapid flushing system, carrying water—probably for respiratory use—to the intestine when the stomach is occupied with food.

The stomach is a spacious thin-walled tube making a clockwise circuit round the lining of the test, to which it is attached in short festoons. The narrower intestine makes a second circuit in reverse direction, then ascends directly to the central anus. The stomach is the seat of digestion and absorption, and is an area of intense phagocytic activity. A full complex of enzymes is secreted by the granular cells of the epithelium. Furthermore, the food is attacked by several sorts of amoebocytes that freely migrate into the lumen through the stomach wall. Red, colourless and green 'granulocytes' cluster round food particles within the lumen, and act as absorbing and distributing units for soluble nutriment which is stored in their granules. Other amoebocytes, known as 'agranulocytes', phagocytose particulate matter which then undergoes intracellular digestion.

Loaded amoebocytes migrate to the lacunae of the haemal system which spread over the gut. By Prussian blue staining, after feeding with iron-containing substances, they can be shown accumulating in the main haemal depots of the body. Engulfment of food by wandering amoebocytes is an efficient method of non-localized intracellular digestion. The haemal system of echinoderms differs from a true blood system in that the transport within it of nutritive and excretory materials takes place in migratory cells in strands of soft tissue, not in fluids pumped through vessels. Distribution of food to the haemal system may also be helped by active absorption of water from the stomach into the haemal spaces giving these an appearance of strong turgor at full digestion.

The intestine and rectum conduct undigested waste to the anus, moving it by intermittent peristaltic waves, and faeces are discharged in loose, rather incoherent strings.

Deposit Feeders 3

3.1 Introduction

The most bulky and apparently un-nutritive of diets are those obtained by animals ingesting the whole substrate. These unselective deposit feeders, as we may call them, are in fact a smaller class than has commonly been thought; almost always some selection is made of the richer organic material at the surface. Thus the lug-worms *Arenicola* appear to swallow entire sand, but get their chief food from the conical head-shaft of their burrow which fills with subsiding deposits from the surface layer. This is rich in diatoms, dinoflagellates, protozoa and much organic debris.

The sand-burrowing worms of the genus *Ophelia* have similar feeding habits. The crowded population of an intertidal beach can pass the whole top 6 in. through their guts in a couple of seasons. The actively burrowing worm, *Sipunculus*, ingests the surface sand with its eversible fringed proboscis. Acorn worms, *Balanoglossus*, also pass voluminous sand castings, yet their feeding does not involve merely the automatic swallowing of sand as they burrow. Glands on the proboscis and collar secrete not only mucus but an amylolytic enzyme, and collected food particles are carried by cilia from the collar to the mouth. Some food is also filtered by the gill slits from the powerful respiratory current in a manner foreshadowing the ciliary feeding of protochordates (see p. 37).

Sea cucumbers or holothurians push the surface deposits into their mouths by means of the circlet of oral tentacles. Largest and most numerous on the coral sand flats of tropical reefs, they feed continuously, passing prolific cylinders and coils of sandy faeces. The first portion of the gut, the tubular stomach, has muscular walls but no particular organs of trituration. Undoubtedly particles are subjected to mutual abrasion and comminution as they rub together during passage through the gut. The walls of the long intestine are surprisingly delicate and thin, and in that sand-burrowing holothurian, the worm-like *Synapta* (Fig. 3–1c), the gut and body wall together resemble merely a transparent sausage casing stretched over the contained column of sand particles. In the sea cucumber the cloaca functions as a respiratory organ, taking in by muscular contractions a constant flow of water to fill the internal gill system of the 'respiratory trees'.

3.2 Deposit-feeding worms

We may look more closely at the gut of deposit-feeding worms (Fig. 3–1a). The lug-worm ingests by everting and withdrawing its short,

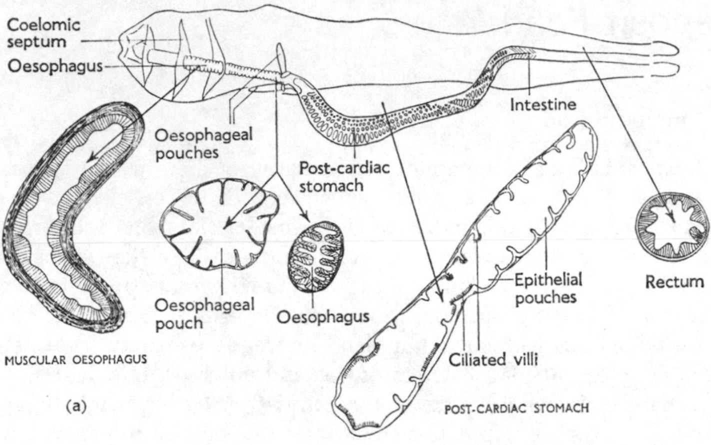

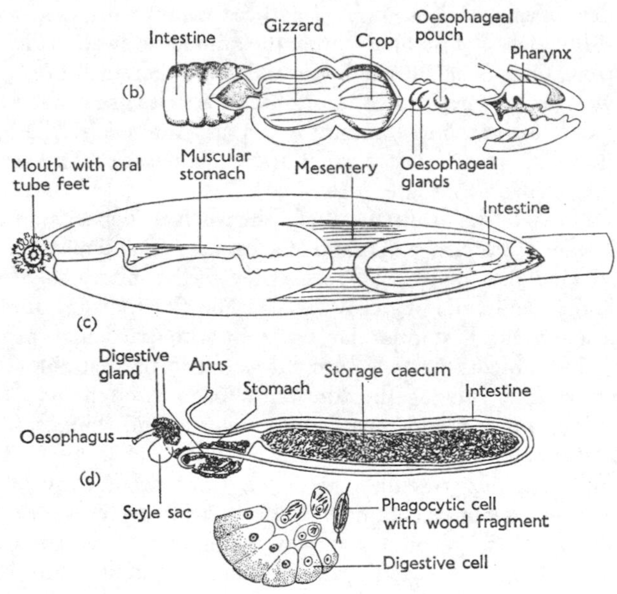

Fig. 3–1 (**a**) Gut of the lug-worm, *Arenicola marina*, with anterior body septa and transverse sections of the various regions. (**b**) Anterior part of the gut of the earthworm, *Lumbricus terrestris*. (**c**) Synaptid holothurian dissected to show the first part of the gut. (**d**) Gut of the wood-boring bivalve, *Teredo navalis*, showing storage caecum and cells of part of digestive gland. (Based on KERMACK (**a**) and POTTS (**d**).)

rounded proboscis. The swallowings are stored temporarily in the short oesophagus and, aided by rhythmic contractions of the body wall, it is this section of the gut that initiates the movement of the food. Two pear-shaped oesophageal pouches open just before the stomach, producing a watery secretion with some amylase. Mixed with this the food passes back in a more fluid state to the stomach, where the gut dilates and its wall is distended with close-set pouches or saccules, bright yellow from chloragogenous tissue. Patches of cilia in the stomach keep the contents well mixed, bringing them in contact with the epithelium of the pouches and with the ciliated, cup-shaped villi which are a feature of the wall between the pouches. The pH within the stomach is depressed to 5·4–6·0 and the principal enzymes are protease and amylase.

It has been estimated that about 96 per cent of the material swallowed is inorganic and of no nutritive value whatever. Large total quantities must thus be put through, and maximum extraction employed; the straight gut of a narrow worm offers little storage space and quick elimination is required to make way for the introduction of fresh swallowings. Faeces are rhythmically voided some 45 minutes after ingestion and, while food is in the stomach, effective means are employed to glean its sparse nutritive content. Enzymes act extracellularly and at the same time particles are engulfed phagocytically by the epithelial cells of the stomach wall. At the base of the epithelium these are taken up by coelomic cells which may carry material into the blood stream or the coelome.

In the intestine, water is absorbed, firmer faeces are produced and temporarily stored in the rectum as cylinders coated and lightly bound with mucus.

In selective deposit feeders and ciliary feeders—as we shall see later—there are complex adaptations for sorting and manipulating the smaller but richer particle flow. In massive deposit swallowers, where the bulk of food is too great, or its nutritive content too sparse, all expedients for sorting have been abandoned.

3·3 Earthworms

The most important terrestrial substrate swallowers are the earthworms of the Lumbricidae, made famous from the studies by Charles Darwin. Where the soils are over-compact the earthworms certainly burrow by eating their way through them, though not all earthworm species have the same feeding habits. *Lumbricus terrestris* most commonly forms a U-shaped burrow from which it protrudes the front end to feed from the surface. Large fragments of dead or fresh organic matter, especially leaves, are drawn down into the burrow. These are moistened in patches by a secretion of alkaline reaction containing an amylase by which starch grains are sometimes externally digested. Pieces may then be torn off the moistened leaf between the prostomium and the lower border of the mouth, or withdrawn into the mouth by the sucking action of the muscular pharynx. In addition, much earthy material is swallowed, of particle size up to 2 mm.

The gut of the earthworm (Fig. 3–1b) begins with a thick-walled dilatable pharynx, having a narrow cavity and strong extrinsic muscles running to the body wall. Behind the pharynx is a short oesophagus into which open, in *Lumbricus*, three pairs of lime-secreting diverticula (one of oesophageal pouches, two of oesophageal 'glands'). Behind the oesophagus the gut widens to a muscular, pear-shaped crop; this storage chamber opens in turn into a spherical gizzard with a strong endowment of muscle. Here, no doubt, as probably elsewhere, particle size is reduced by rubbing and abrasion. The gizzard leads back into the long, straight intestine, with its secreting and absorbing surface increased by a large typhlosolar fold. Movement of gut contents is mainly peristaltic, though the lining cells are ciliated and interspersed with mucus goblets.

The faeces are voided in *Lumbricus*, though not in all earthworms, in the well-known surface casts. Charles Darwin calculated that the cast-making earthworms bring to the surface 1–25 tons of soil per acre per year by their feeding activities. In soils of good pasture land there is commonly a stone-free layer 4–8 inches deep and it has been estimated that the top 4 inches pass through the alimentary tract of earthworms in 11½ years where there is a high population. By selecting and triturating organic particles, the worms bring about a large and intimate mixture of new organic debris with the soil. In comparison with the soil, worm casts have more total and more nitrate nitrogen, more total and exchangeable calcium, more exchangeable potassium and magnesium, more available phosphate, more organic carbon and a greater base exchange capacity. The casts are also more nearly neutral in reaction than the original surface soil, sometimes 75 per cent more so. This is apparently due to the alkaline secretions of the gut as a whole, rather than to the particular output of the calciferous glands which produce crystals of largely inactive calcite and are said to be primarily excretory in their role.

3·4 Wood-borers and swallowers

Two marine borers making galleries in submerged timber may be classed among the substrate swallowers, in that they ingest large instalments of wood-shavings and have evolved an enzyme capable of hydrolysing the cellulose fraction of the wood. The timber-boring isopod crustacean, *Limnoria*, produces this enzyme in its digestive diverticula. In the aberrant lamellibranch mollusc, *Teredo*, ingested wood is stored in a long caecum of the stomach, unrepresented in other bivalves (Fig. 3–1d). Amoebocytic cells, in a special region of the digestive diverticula, ingest wood particles which are then attacked by an intracellular cellulase. In this way, particles may be utilized which are too large to be phagocytosed by the digestive gland epithelial cells directly; the amoebocytes afterwards disintegrate or with their digested contents are absorbed by the epithelium.

Carnivores 4

4.1 Carnivores in various phyla

The rewards of a carnivorous life are nutritively rich. Muscle and other proteins are among the most compact and economic of foods; but, easy though it may be to assimilate, the single unit of animal food frequently requires great expenditure of energy to catch and immobilize. If the prey unit is too small it is scarcely worth the expense of catching; being of economic catch size, it is certain to be bulky to swallow, and hence many carnivores take intermittent, over-large meals, and are apt to enter upon a quiescent period of digestion.

The problem of bulk may be overcome in one of three ways: by a mouth and fore-gut distensible and capacious enough to take in a meal at one massive swallowing; by teeth employed not only for prehension but for shearing and dismembering; and by reducing the prey to a liquid form with enzymes acting outside the body, so that the gut is presented simply with a rich protein broth.

In contrast with problems of pursuit, sedentary food may be difficult of access through being enclosed in heavy shells or exoskeletons. Such hard casings may be crushed by toothed or muscular gizzards after swallowing whole, or, with more subtlety, the shells may be bored through or entered by narrow chinks and the food taken out in small fragments. The most important group of externally digesting carnivores are undoubtedly the Arachnida, which are so uniformly adapted for this habit that we may best consider them among 'Fluid Feeders'.

The earliest metazoan carnivores massively swallow the prey, just as an *Amoeba* or a carnivorous ciliate will engulf a living flagellate. The Coelenterata, nearly all carnivores, reduce the prey to possession by grappling it with the tentacles after contact with stinging cells or nematoblasts. The food is then pushed or held against the mouth with the tentacles and engulfed by the contraction of the circular pharyngeal muscles. The whole body cavity or *coelenteron* is generally held to serve as a 'gut' but in the largest of the polypes, the anemones, a special investment of active digestive epithelium closes around the body of the prey. After feeding *Calliactis parasitica* with coloured gelatin blocks, the food bolus below the stomodaeum was found to be completely invested with closely adhering mesenteric filaments (Fig. 4–1a). These structures are the glandular edges of the radial folds or mesenteries that divide up the coelenteron; they are clad with both secreting and absorbing cells, and move actively over the bolus, each lifting off and being replaced with another as its cells become engorged with food. Secretion of a powerful protease, stimulated by protein food, initiates contact digestion at the epithelial surface. The food mass shrinks and dissolves as the filaments press upon it, and waste is defaecated in a compact mucus-coated pellet by contractile movements of the column. The remainder of the coelenteron may simultaneously act as a respiratory organ, water entering it freely by the ciliated gutters or *siphonoglyphs* running down either side of the inturned sleeve of the mouth, or stomodaeum.

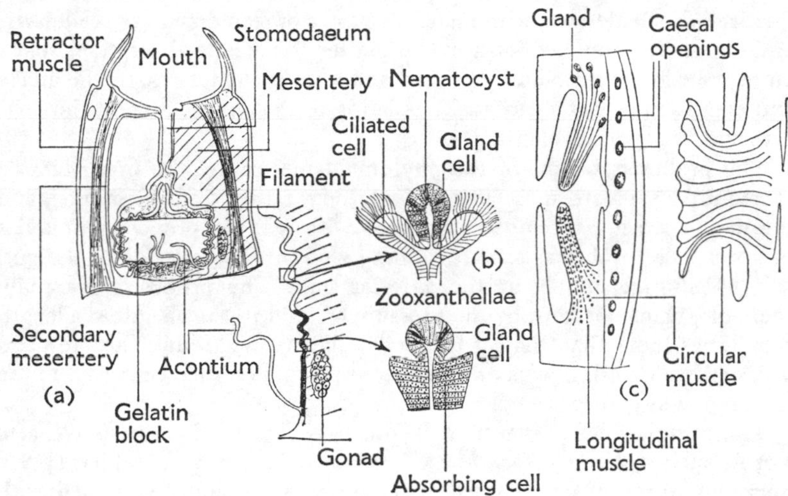

Fig. 4–1 (**a**) Diagrammatic vertical section of an anemone fed with a gelatin block, showing the disposition of the mesenteric filament. (**b**) Histological details of the ciliated and glandular portion of the filament. (**c**) Sagittal section of the mouth, pharynx and stomach of a polyclad turbellarian, showing (right) the bell-shaped pharynx everted.

An analogous temporary 'stomach' of separate digestive units encloses the food of some siphonophores, such as the Portuguese man-o'-war, *Physalia*. Prey captured with the long fishing tentacles, or dactylozooids, is drawn up and held close beneath the float. It is then invested by the trumpet mouths of 100 or more gastrozooid polypes, adhering like little suckers and pouring upon it a supply of proteolytic enzyme.

Like the coelenterates, the free-living flatworms or Turbellaria have a gut with no separate anus. We may take as a simple example a freshwater triclad, *Planaria* or *Polycelis*, with a gut divisible into three blind branches and opening by an invaginable tubular pharynx. The mouth lies not in its conventional position on the head, but on the under-surface two-thirds of the way back—a convenient site to enable the flatworm to invest soft prey or thrust the pharynx straight down into the food mass (Fig. 4–1c).

In the marine polyclad flatworms such as *Leptoplana*, the gut surface is greatly increased by repeatedly branching outgrowths, leading from a central 'stomach', so-called. This space and the larger branches are ciliated; in the smaller branches the lining is glandular and absorptive, while at the periphery the gut branches may anastomose in an intricately circulating system. In many species of polyclads, the pharynx is bell-like and extrusible, with a frilled muscular edge that may close securely upon small worms and crustaceans and other living prey. Digestion is initiated by glands opening into the pharynx itself; later events resemble the sequence in coelenterates, with materials partly broken down extracellularly, and digestion completed intracellularly after particulate absorption. When empty, the gut is periodically flushed out, as in coelenterates, by the intake and expulsion of water, no doubt assisting in the oxygenation of the delicate and very permeable tissues.

The proboscis worms of the phylum Nemertea are the first Metazoa to acquire a separate anus. The gut is a long, rather featureless tube, and the most characteristic organ associated with it is the proboscis: this lies in a muscular proboscis sheath running along the dorsal side of the gut, and opening separately at the anterior end. The proboscis is rapidly eversible, being shot out by the pressure of fluid in the sheath to a length sometimes more than that of the body. It entwines round the prey and immobilizes it with mucus or other secretions, to be then conveyed to the mouth and swallowed entire.

The same mode of ingestion is practised by carnivorous polychaete worms such as *Nereis*, *Nephthys*, *Glycera* and *Eunice*, all of which have a muscular introvert or pharynx, with its eversible lining equipped with small teeth. In the sea-mouse, *Aphrodite*, the pharynx is a heavily muscular tube with a narrow lumen, and serves as a gizzard for crushing animal food.

Among the carnivorous echinoderms, the starfishes (Asteroidea) frequently digest the prey externally by everting the stomach over it and pouring out a supply of proteolytic enzymes (Fig. 4–2). The long-armed stars of the family Asteroidea feed chiefly upon bivalve molluscs. The shell

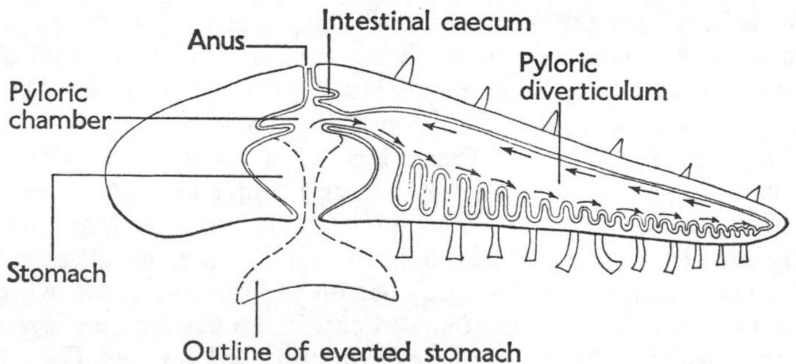

Fig. 4–2 Diagrammatic vertical section of a starfish, *Asterias*, showing the regions of the gut and its diverticula.

is wrenched open by the suction power of the multiple tube feet, applied relentlessly until the adductor muscle of the bivalve relaxes from fatigue. The stomach is then extruded as a thin collapsible bag and inserted into the slightly gaping shell; it can be stretched to a great capacity and is finally withdrawn through the mouth, filled with liquefied and partly digested food. Most of the space within the central disc of the star is filled by this bag. Opening from it above is a smaller pyloric chamber with a short, narrow intestine leading directly upwards to the aboral surface. Digestion is completed by the enzymes from the pyloric caeca, a pair of long, much folded glandular diverticula extending into each of the five—or more—arms. Enzymes are carried to the stomach by outward ciliary currents while along the opposite wall, ingoing currents being soluble material into the caeca for absorption. Large indigestible waste is voided through the mouth, small fragments through the anus.

Many of the carnivorous gastropods specialize in swallowing whole prey. The flat-bodied opisthobranch *Philine*, which burrows in sand, crushes the shells of small bivalves in an oesophageal gizzard. This forms a rectangular box with muscular walls and large calcified internal teeth.

The cone shells are noted for the sudden capture and swallowing of moving prey, including blennies, gobies and other small fish. A neurotoxin from the salivary glands is injected into the prey by the special harpoon-like radular teeth. There is no odontophore, and the radular caecum is bent at a sharp angle; each limb contains a sheaf of slender teeth, barbed at the tips. The shaft forms a partly closed tube, conveying the poison from the opening of the salivary duct. The toxin of the geography cone (*Conus geographus*) and several others has at times proved fatal to man.

The quarry is located by the chemoreceptors of the osphradium, leading

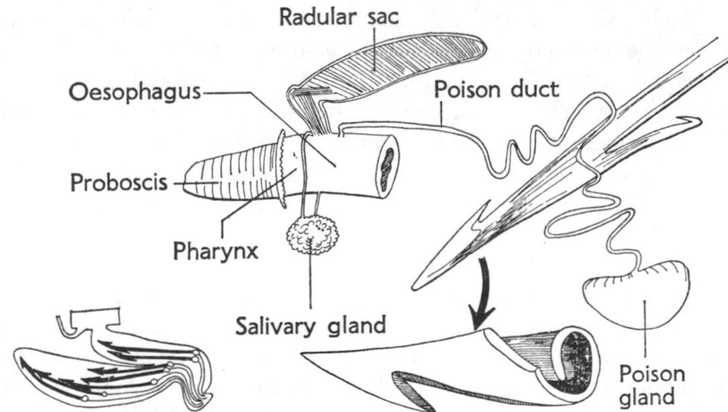

Fig. 4–3 Anterior part of gut of *Conus striatus*. The terminal part of a single tooth is shown superimposed with, below, an enlargement of the grooved barb. Lower left is a diagram of the teeth in the radular sac.

the cone to crawl towards it and 'cover' it with the poised proboscis. With each successful strike a single harpoon is shot out and lodged. Its struggles quelled, the whole fish is smoothly engulfed into the distensible proboscis sheath. Rapid proteolytic digestion follows as the first part of the prey is passed into the oesophagus, and with the progress of digestion the whole mass is softened and received into the fore-gut.

The most prodigious swallowers are probably to be found among some of the deep-sea fish. In the small black lantern fish *Melanocoetus* (Fig. 4–4a)

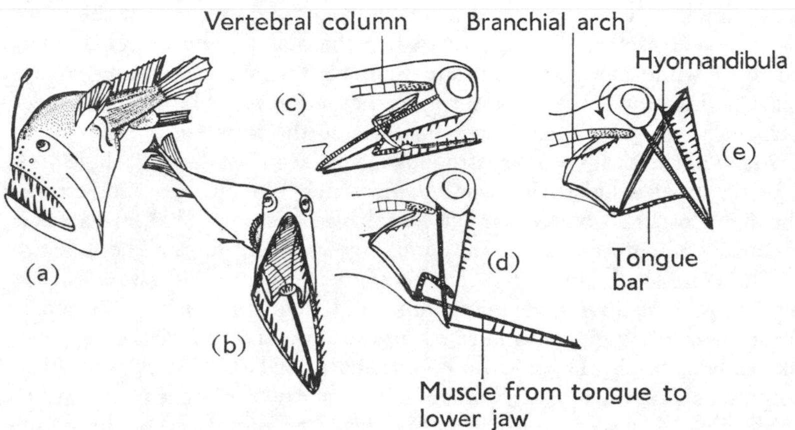

Fig. 4–4 Some large-mouthed deep sea fish: **(a)** the angler fish, *Melanocoetus cirrifer;* **(b)** *Malacosteus indicus* with the gape fully open; **(c–e)** stages in the opening and closing of the jaws.

the wide vertical mouth and the great bag of the throat dominate the whole design of the body. The gulper eels, *Eurypharynx*, have the jaws grotesquely underslung; the mouth opens chiefly by the dropping of the lower jaw with its own weight, and the closing musculature is also weak. But the mouth forms a huge receptacle that can be widened by spreading the jaw framework sideways to engulf prey far larger than the predator.

A still more bizarre design of the mouth is shown by the deep-water stomatioid fish, *Malacosteus indicus* (Fig. 4–4b). The jaws are slender struts with the angle carried well back below the body. By the contraction of special muscle bands they can be swung open and forward with great speed, and the lower jaw can snap suddenly at a passing animal, like the mask of a predatory dragon-fly. The sharp fang teeth strike into the prey as the jaw is swung backwards. It is then thrown into the spacious framework of the mouth as the jaws snap shut. The skin of the whole back and floor of the mouth has disappeared, removing a water resistance that would be too great for the closing of the jaws. The only framework behind the jaws is of the lateral hyoid bones and the narrow muscle band to the interangle of the mandibles.

4.2 Cephalopoda

These molluscs are pre-eminent for their high tempo of life, both in their jet locomotion and their fast capture and digestion of food. In the squid, *Loligo*, taking small fish, or the cuttle-fish, *Sepia*, feeding on shrimps, the prey is secured by the lightning extension of the two tentacular arms, normally kept ensheathed. The octopus by contrast pounces on crabs and similar prey with its outspread arms and inter-arm web.

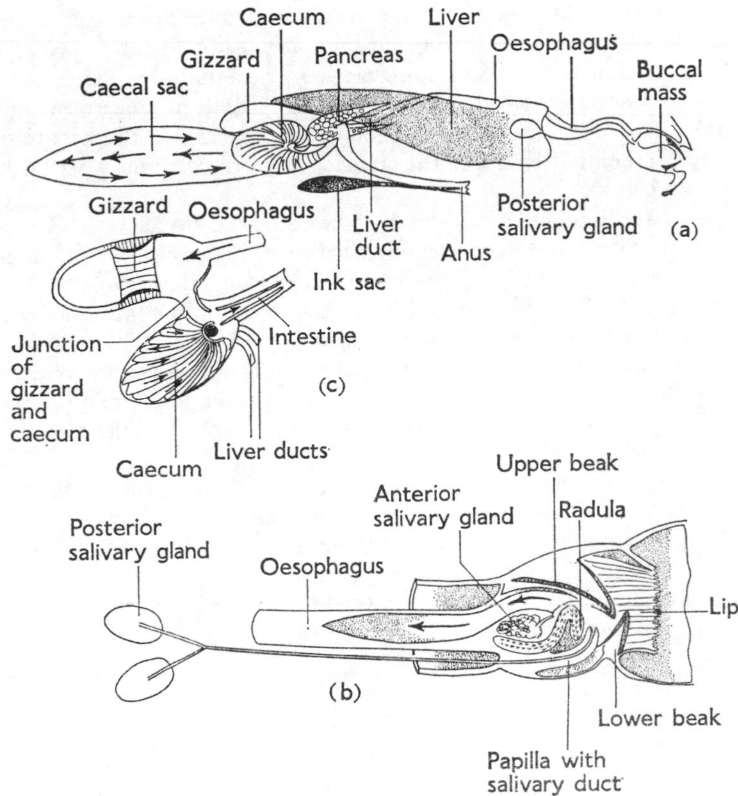

Fig. 4–5 The cephalopod gut: **(a)** the alimentary canal of *Loligo;* **(b)** the buccal mass and its glands of *Sepia;* **(c)** diagram of the stomach of *Sepia*, in longitudinal section. (**(a)** after BIDDER.)

In all cephalopods the prey is held against the mouth by the circlet of suckered arms and its struggles are stilled by the injection of a toxin from the posterior salivary glands. In the octopus this contains tyramine, octopamine and hydroxytryptamine, having a powerful effect on the nervous system. The food is bitten into small pieces by the horny parrot-like beak, aided by strokes of the small radula. Powerful salivary proteases are injected from the salivary glands and the food is reduced to a semi-pulpy condition before being cleaned out from the exoskeleton and carried down the oesophagus to the stomach.

The alimentary canal of *Loligo* is represented in Fig. 4–5a. The oesophagus is narrow and muscular and the stomach is a large contractile bag, capable of vigorous peristalsis. It serves as a gizzard where food is thoroughly churned and subjected to preliminary digestion. A narrow isthmus from the stomach leads to the caecum, a thin-walled sac forming an annexe to the ducts from the digestive glands and also leading to the opening of the intestine. The Cephalopoda possess two sorts of digestive gland, known rather inappropriately as 'liver' and 'pancreas'. Both produce proteolytic and amylolytic enzymes. The secretion of the pancreas is the first to become active, being driven into the stomach from the caecum where it has been stored.

After early digestion for an hour or more in the stomach, food is released in instalments to the caecum where it remains up to four hours. Digestion is completed by the action of 'liver' secretion. Resistant solid particles are all the while removed from the caecum to the intestine by the action of the ciliated organ of the caecal wall. This is a set of converging folds and leaflets with currents directed towards the intestine. With the nutrient fluid cleared of all solid remains, absorption of soluble products takes place in the large, thin-walled caecal sac. At intervals the remaining residue in the caecum is voided to the intestine.

An intricate arrangement of valves and channels keeps these different functions segregated and properly phased. The efficiency of the cephalopod gut lies in its rapidity of digestive action; this can be renewed whenever food is available, while the processing of a previous meal is allowed to go on at the same time.

4·3 Crustacea

The largest and most advanced of the Crustacea, the crayfish and crabs and lobsters, form a contrast in many ways to the Cephalopoda. Though some of them are fleet of foot, they are all benthic rather than fast-swimming, and they feed on an indiscriminate range of slow prey. Small animals, such as worms and molluscs, and dead tissues are pushed to the mouth by a complex battery of limbs and are finally seized and ingested by the heavy mandibles. The fore-gut incorporates a complex system of mincers and filters; the mouth parts are an apparatus designed for thoroughness rather than speed.

As in all arthropods, the crustacean gut begins with a large chitinized stomodaeum and terminates with a proctodaeum, both ectodermal. In between, and derived from the endoderm, is the mid-gut or mesenteron.

A short oesophagus leads directly up to the stomach, which is the site of internal trituration, pressing and filtering the food in preparation for absorption by the digestive gland. Forming part of the stomodaeum, the stomach has a chitinous lining throughout its two parts, the larger 'cardiac' chamber in front and the smaller 'pyloric' chamber behind. Near the junction of these chambers, the stomach roof is occupied by a gastric mill, a set of lining plates and heavy teeth formed by the local thickening of the chitin. The pyloric chamber incorporates a mid-gut filter, a filter press and a gland filter; the last-named guards on either side the aperture of the digestive gland, which is a soft and very extensive yellow-brown mass, built up of fine tubules packed around and behind the stomach. The crustacean digestive gland, like that of the Mollusca, is not only absorptive but secretory; its epithelium has, however, separate cells subserving each role. In the crayfish, proteolytic, amylolytic and lipolytic enzymes are passed outwards from the follicles of the gland to flow back along the ventral pyloric channels to the cardiac chamber. They enter this region at either side along the comb-fringed ventrolateral grooves, continuous with the ventral channels. Extracellular digestion takes place here and most of the soluble products flow back through the gland filter and into the digestive

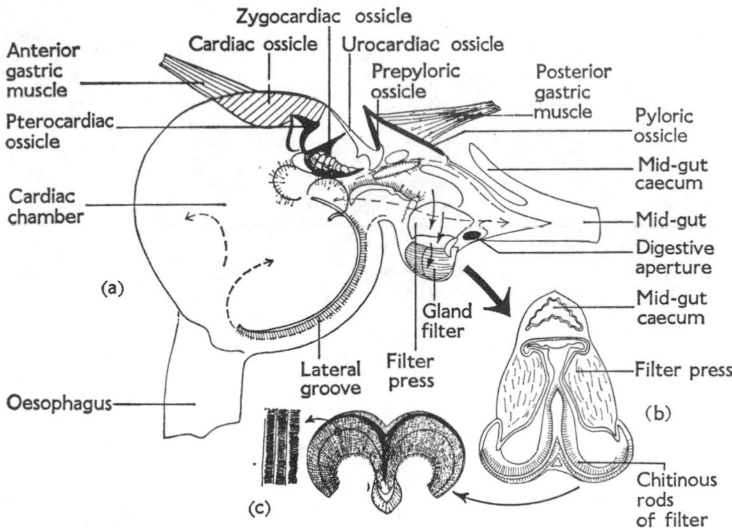

Fig. 4–6 The stomach of the Norway lobster, *Nephrops norvegicus:* (**a**) the cardiac and pyloric chambers in sagittal section; (**b**) cross section of the region of the filter press and gland filter; (**c**) detail of the gland filter (removed) and of its chitinous rods. (After YONGE.)

diverticula for absorption. A small and subsidiary amount of absorption occurs in the straight mid-gut, or in the short caeca from it.

The ossicles of the gastric mill are shown in Fig. 4–6. The prepyloric and pyloric plates are freely hinged and, by the action of anterior and posterior gastric muscles attaching to the stomach, the median tooth and the two strong lateral teeth are brought together, breaking up anything lying between them. The anterior part of the pyloric chamber is guarded from the cardiac chamber by a massive cardiopyloric valve, covered with bristle-like setae. Material fine enough to pass this valve may proceed by a dorsal channel, the mid-gut filter, straight to the mid-gut. Much of it, however, seeps downwards between the two heavy side walls, forming the filter press, and after further trituration enters the ventrally placed gland filter. This structure consists of two semicircular plates, concave dorsally and united in the middle line. Attached to the anterior border and free behind like the teeth of an excessively fine comb are a series of chitinous rods, each in turn bearing hair-like setae. Dissolved material that has passed the gland filter is carried into the digestive gland for absorption. The residue is carried up into the press and finally to the mid-gut.

Filter Feeders 5

Filter feeding, by the straining of fine particles from suspension in the water, is resorted to by most of the sessile marine invertebrates. In one group, the barnacles or Cirripedia, food is collected by a casting net of setal fringed limbs swept through the water by active muscular work. But in most filter feeders, including the sponges, the polyzoans and brachiopods, the ascidians, the bivalves and some gastropods and polychaete worms, food gathering proceeds almost wholly by the use of cilia and mucus.

Filter feeding is a continuous process, though achieved with great economy of energy. The suspended food may consist of an almost pure plant diet, as of diatoms and dinoflagellates, though more often of small naked flagellates; or it may include zooplankton and varying elements of organic debris such as dead parts and faeces, and even grains of sand. But whether pure or mingled with material less nutritive, food in suspension is very diffuse, and great volumes of water must be driven through the meshes of the different kinds of filters. The oyster, for example passes thirty times its volume of water through its gills in one hour.

Suspended food, unlike the prey of carnivores, is widespread and automatically obtained. Water currents are set up and drawn from a wide area through filtering screens; the material so concentrated is generally bound into ropes or boluses with mucus—a multitude of small unruly particles would be no sooner collected than dispersed. Current production is the work of powerful flexuous cilia. The particles are sometimes entrapped by stiff, inert comb-like cilia, more often by a lattice-like spread of mucus, and sometimes by both together.

Filtering is generally carried out by specialized structures lying outside the gut, before the mouth is reached, such as the tentacle crown of tube worms, the lophophore of polyzoa and the ctenidia of bivalve molluscs. These need not closely concern us here. However, in one important group of filter feeders, the protochordates, the filtering organs are located within the gut, consisting of an enlarged and specialized pharynx that overshadows in complexity all the rest of the digestive tract.

Both the sea-squirts (Ascidiacea) and Amphioxus have a variant of the same type of filtering pharynx. Opening by the mouth in front and leading to the oesophagus behind, this branchial sac is fenestrated with small openings called *stigmata*, perforating the pharynx and the body wall essentially as do the gill slits of a fish. The stigmata are, however, finally subdivided and crossed by horizontal connecting bars to form an open lattice work. The body wall being consequently weakened at this level, a fold of integument called the atrium encloses the space where the slits open. With the atrial cavity laid open, the pharyngeal wall looks somewhat like a limp Aertex singlet. Water drawn in at the mouth is passed through the stigmata to the atrial cavity by current-driving lateral cilia situated along side walls. Particles are strained off and retained within the pharynx by a sheet of mucus that covers the interior surface as a permeable mesh. The mucus is produced by gland cells in the ventrical longitudinal groove known as the endostyle; by the action of a median fringe of long cilia at the bottom of the groove, it is wafted outwards in two continuous lateral sheets; other cilia carry it up the sides of the pharynx to the dorsal hyperbranchial groove which runs back to the oesophagus. In many ascidians the movement of mucus is assisted also by the movement of longitudinal folds within the pharynx pushing it like a long broom, with small ciliated papillae acting like brushes. In the hyperbranchial groove a rope of the collected food is fashioned, being held by the ciliated tongues or plain lamina curving round the groove from one side. Backwardly-beating cilia help to carry the food rope to the oesophagus.

The gut behind the pharynx is very simple. The role of the stomach is to receive the food string and make its mucus less viscous by the lowered pH of the medium. As in all ciliary feeders this is the site where the food load is shed, with individual particles set free for digestion and absorption. The enzymes include protease, amylase and lipase acting extracellularly. They are secreted from special cells in the stomach lining or (in some ascidians) in small diverticula. In the intestine, where the pH rises to more than 7, viscosity of the mucus again increases and a firm string is reconstituted from those particles that are left. By ciliary movements this string is carried repeatedly back and forth across the typhlosole as it passes through the intestine. With fresh accretions of mucus it is fashioned into an elegant faecal rope, firm enough to be discharged from the anus without fouling the ingoing current.

In ascidians the food string is grasped and thrust backwards by oblique ciliated ridges in the oesophagus. In the lancelet, or Amphioxus, the traction power is exerted from behind by the short section of the intestine known as the ileo-colon ring (Fig. 5–1). Here strong cilia twist the string into a tight spiral coil and rotate it under moderate tension. The rest of the gut lining is largely set free for other tasks. A dorsal by-pass through the ileo-colon ring allows direct passage to the posterior intestine, while at intervals small pieces of the rotating mucus rope are nipped off and compacted into faeces.

An important feature of the gut of Amphioxus is the digestive diverticulum, running forward from the stomach, alongside the pharynx. The term hepatopancreas should not be applied to this organ: it has none of the functions of the liver which is quite unrepresented in protochordates. A pancreatic role it must, however, be allowed, since it produces a tryptic protease, a lipase and an amylase. The deep-staining, large-nucleated digestive cells are clearly the homologues of those in ascidians, and have been shown by E. W. Barrington to bear a detailed resemblance with the exocrine secreting cells of the pancreas in the higher vertebrate series.

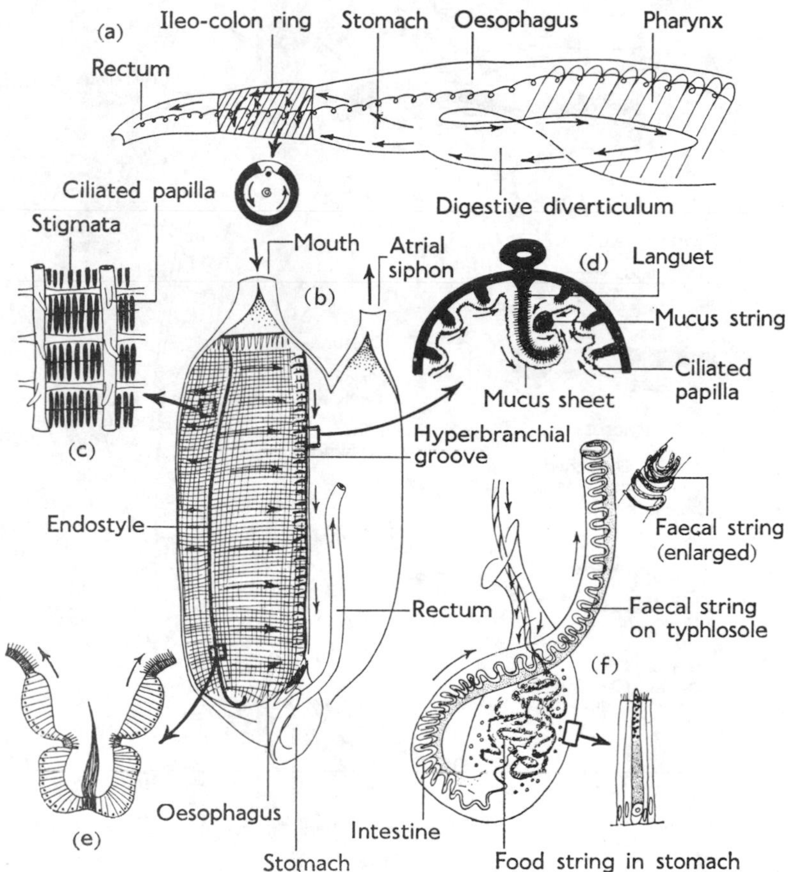

Fig. 5–1 The gut of protochordates: (**a**) diagram of the alimentary canal of amphioxus, *Branchiostoma lanceolatum*, with section of ileo-colon ring; (**b**) *Ciona intestinalis*, alimentary canal with branchial sac opened, and with details of (**c**) pharynx wall with stigmata, (**d**) hyperbranchial groove and mucus string, and (**e**) endostyle; (**f**) *Ciona intestinalis*, oesophagus, stomach and intestine, with contained food string, and details of digestive cells and folded faecal string. (From BARRINGTON (**a**) and MILLAR (**d**).)

The Polyzoa are another group of ciliary feeders using a rotating rod of mucus or faeces to manipulate food particles. The tiny gut of an ectoproct polypide (Fig. 5–2a) forms an exquisite mechanism that can sometimes be seen by transparency in the intact animal. Food entering the stomach in

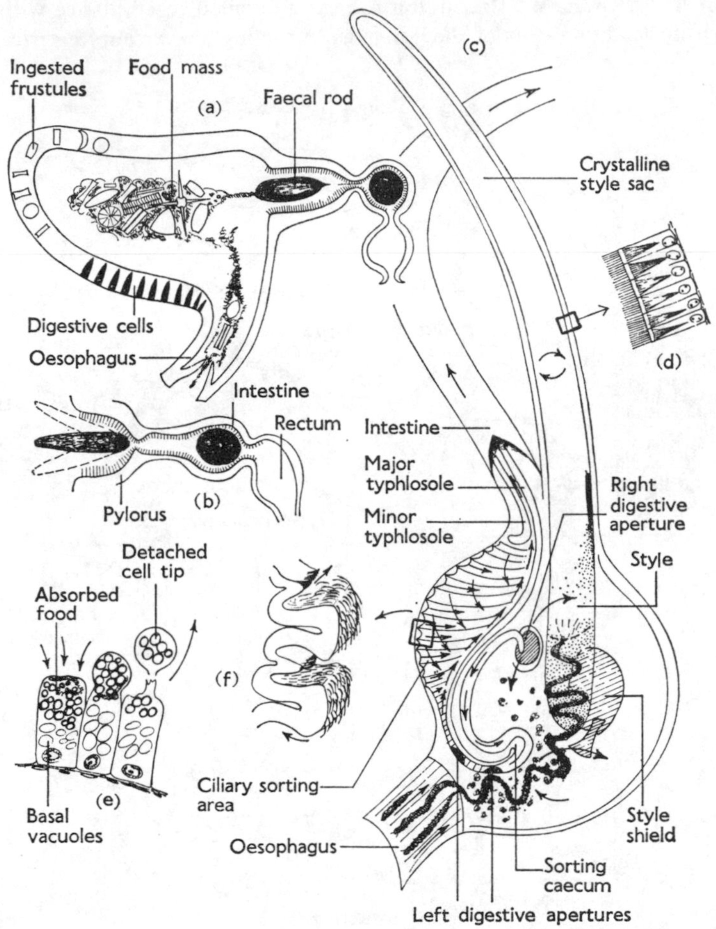

Fig. 5–2 The gut of a polyzoan and a bivalve: **(a)** diagrammatic longitudinal section of the stomach and intestine of an ectoproct polyzoan; **(b)** sketch showing changes in swivelling axis of the faecal rod; **(c)** stomach and crystalline style sac of the oyster, *Ostrea edulis*, with details of **(d)** style sac epithelium, **(e)** digestive gland cells, and **(f)** ciliary sorting area.

the mucus string is engaged by a small swivelling rod, projecting from a thimble-like pylorus, in which it is continually rotated by cilia, at up to 70 turns a minute. The rod points alternately towards the stomach entry where it engages more mucus string with food, and into the large bulb of the stomach where particles are detached and stirred and brought under the action of enzymes. As well as containing gland cells, the stomach lining is freely absorptive and can even phagocytose large diatoms. At intervals the pylorus may open out flat and suck back the rotating rod into the intestine. Another is gradually built up to replace it, and the rejected rod is kneaded into a faecal pellet in the intestine. Turned by the lining cilia as on a lathe, the pellets are given a final coat of mucus and forcibly expelled from the anus.

The rotating rod of the gut in ciliary feeders has been called by the author the 'ergatula' from a Greek word meaning a little capstan. Its function (as we have seen) is to concentrate the work of transport at some special part of the gut; and it is found at its highest development in the Mollusca in which it has acquired other important roles as well. In the bivalve stomach, and among some gastropods, the rotating rod is known as a crystalline style. No longer constructed of faeces, it now forms a column of flexible, hyaline mucoprotein, long, tapering and semitransparent. It projects into the stomach from a special sac, the style caecum, which has originated as part of the first section of the intestine, but now in most bivalves lies alongside but completely cut off from the intestine.

The stomach of a bivalve (Fig. 5–2c–f) is far more complex than that of a polyzoan or protochordate, and to understand its structure we must remember that bottom-dwelling bivalves take into the gut a far more mixed flow of debris which requires extensive sorting before final digestion can take place. The winnowing out of the coarse and indigestible from the fine and organic is, of course, more important in those molluscs relying on the surface detrital mantle as their food, less so where the food is a more pure suspension filtered mainly from the water above.

Food is collected by the gill and undergoes preliminary sorting by the labial palps. The mucus strings entering the stomach by the short oesophagus are caught up by the rotating head of the style as it projects from its caecum. The ends of the strings are wound on to the style and rotated with it; they are thrown into a tight coil which in turn draws more material out of the oesophagus. As the string enters, its slack is taken up by progressive winding into the style. Meanwhile the mucus becomes less viscid by the effect of the lowered pH of the stomach; food particles are shed and the string itself may be reduced to an axial thread, usually keeping a slender continuity with the style.

The rotating crystalline style is not only a capstan, but acts too as a pestle; it stirs the particles shed from the food string repeatedly over the grooved and ciliated part of the lining of the stomach. This structure forms a ciliary sorting area and separates particles into coarse and lighter fractions. Sorting areas are important in all molluscs, and sometimes they may be extended out of the stomach into a shallow sorting caecum; one such diverticulum is shown in Fig. 5–2c of the oyster's stomach. A typhlosole winds its way into and out of the caecum, and multiple openings of the digestive gland occur there. The coarsest material resulting from sorting is conducted along a ciliated groove, bounded by the typhlosole, directly into the first part of the intestine. The finer particles still remaining undergo some extracellular digestion in the stomach by the action of enzymes coming from two sources: from the detached tips of the cells of the digestive diverticula, and from a powerful amylase liberated from the style as its head becomes softened and dissolved in the weakly acid medium of the stomach. As well as being rotated by powerful cilia, the style is also thrust slowly into the stomach by cilia beating longitudinally towards the opening of the style sac. As it gradually dissolves it is simultaneously renewed by fresh secretion in the caecum, and maintains its constant length as it is pushed downward. Thus, as well as being a capstan and a pestle, the style also serves as an enzyme store—an ideal mechanism for the slow, continuous liberation of small quantities of amylase. The same enzyme comes from the digestive gland, with the addition of protease and lipase.

Particles are absorbed in two ways. The largest digestible material, such as diatoms, may be engulfed by amoebocytic cells that make their way in from the blood spaces beneath the stomach lining. These are especially noteworthy in the oyster where, with the phagocytosed contents, they may retreat into the epithelium or break up to be finally absorbed themselves. Fine food is ultimately taken up by the cells of the digestive diverticula, and digestion is completed intracellularly.

The digestive diverticula have paired, or secondarily more numerous openings from the stomach. They branch and rebranch to form a bulky greenish-brown gland, sometimes inappropriately called the 'liver'. The cells of the terminal lobules resemble those of the gastropod digestive gland (see p. 19): they are by turns absorptive and secretory, and when their tips break asunder they carry both enzyme granules and excretory matter to the stomach.

The intestine of the bivalve is only moderately long; its role is to divide up the mucus string of waste coming from the stomach and fashion short sections into faecal pellets. These are rounded off and enveloped with clear mucus for final discharge into the mantle cavity.

A number of large vertebrates feed by specialized filtering methods; not that their food is generally of diatoms, but of the much larger zooplankton, including—in the whales—the shrimp-like crustaceans known as euphausiids.

At the smaller level of size, the tadpoles of many frogs and toads are entirely microphagous, while others take the bulk of their food from the water currents passing through their gill filters. Their filtering habit is entirely distinct in its origin from that of protochordates, and the mechanisms are indeed very different in detail. The inhalant current is no longer created by cilia, but the gill pouches develop filters through which water is pumped by muscular action. Most tadpoles still use the jaws for masticatory ingestion, but in the mountain frog *Ascaphus* the tadpole's mouth is preoccupied as a holding sucker and the nostrils are used for the feeding and respiratory current. Fig. 5–3a shows a longitudinal section of the mouth and pharynx of a tadpole of *Bufo bufo*. The pharynx is wide and flat so that water is drawn through it as a thin sheet. In front of the gill openings it is partly divided by oblique septa called the dorsal and ventral vela. Water leaving the pharynx passes ventrally through the gill openings which are guarded by lattice-like filters forming a grating that holds back larger particles. Most of the particulate food is, however, thrown towards the oesophagus by centrifugal force, where the water turns through an angle of 180° behind the vela. Mucus is secreted in grooves on either side behind the dorsal velum, and the two food strings so formed are twisted together as they pass down the oesophagus.

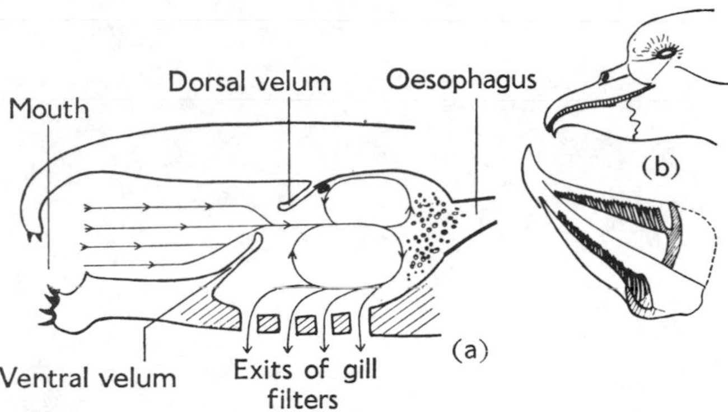

Fig. 5–3 (**a**) Diagram of longitudinal section of the pharynx of a tadpole of *Bufo*, showing the movement of water currents and particles. (**b**) Head and upper jaw of the broad-billed prion, *Pachyptila forsteri*, showing the filtering lamellae. ((**a**) from SAVAGE.)

Of the marine birds, the leading plankton filterers are the broad-billed prions, *Pachyptila* (Fig. 5–3b). In these the upper part of the bill bears two rows of comb-like lamellae through which skimmed-up plankton is strained; the large fleshy tongue acts as a plunger. Among freshwater birds, the duck tribe have a set of simple bill lamellae or side-strainers. In the flamingoes the gill is developed to a filter of the highest pitch of efficiency. Dr. Penelope Jenkins has given us a detailed study of its structure and function, and has shown how two African flamingo species can co-exist on the same lakes without competing for food. The small *Phoeniconaias minor* sweeps the bill through the surface water and filters out blue green algae and diatoms. The larger *Phoenicopterus antiquorum* has a coarser filter with which it feeds in the bottom muds on chironomid larvae and other small invertebrates.

Among the pelagic fish, the herring and the mackerel possess long thin gill-rakers which prevent the escape of copepods and other zooplankton. Some of the largest of the sharks, the basking-shark *Cetorhinus* and the whale-shark *Rhinodon*, feed solely on plankton, strained by similar gill rakers. In the whalebone whales, Mystacoceti, the well-known filtering apparatus consists of close-set transverse plates, up to 300 in right whales. As the lower jaw is raised and the tongue is brought close to the root of the mouth, euphausiid shrimps or 'krill' are strained off by the finely-divided, horny fringes of the baleen plates.

Fluid Feeders 6

Almost every kind of plant and animal fluid may be used as food: cell sap or the watery tissues of plants, productions such as nectar or honeydew, the exudates of decay, and the wide variety of liquids and secretions of animals—blood, protein-rich coelomic fluid, egg yolk and albumen, even sweat which is sucked up by butterflies for its salt content. In most such diets the constituents will tend to be pure and fairly easily digestible; the main problems to be surmounted are those of gaining access to fluids in other living organisms, of pumping or sucking them into the gut, and of storing their inevitably large bulk. Where the food is blood, there is the additional problem of preventing coagulation; as well as an anticoagulant the saliva sometimes contains an irritant which promotes the supply of blood to the area being sampled.

Not a few animals that live on body fluids have simplified the whole problem of intake by lying immersed in nutritive fluids and absorbing them straight through the surface of the body. The outer body wall then does duty as a gut, as in the cestode flatworms and in degenerate parasitic barnacles such as *Sacculina*, and even in one entoparasitic gastropod, *Enteroxenos*, living in holothurians.

6.1 Insects

We may begin with those forms feeding on plant fluids, taking a first example from the insect order Hemiptera. These numerous insects, broadly known as 'bugs', are all suctorial whether on plant or animal food. The piercing stylets are the long flexible mandibles and maxillae; these converge closely as they pass down the groove in the labium or instrument guide. The two maxillae form together a narrower tube for injection of saliva and a wider channel for sucking up food. In a sap feeder such as a coccid, the oesophagus is a simple narrow tube. As in many fluid feeders the mid-gut has lost its peritrophic membrane, protection against hard particles being no longer needed. The stomach (Fig. 6–1c) is formed by the greatly dilated mid-gut, separated by a sphincter from the long intestine. The most interesting feature of the stomach is the part known as the *filter chamber*. The first and third portions of the mid-gut form extensive coils which lie against each other, enveloped in a fold of the rectum and invisible from the body cavity. The middle part lies free and its histology is very distinct, with vacuolated and secretory cells. Such a topography clearly allows excess fluid to pass from the first to the third part of the mid-gut directly. The middle part, being short-circuited, receives for digestion and absorption only the valuable constitutents left after removal of fluid.

Enzyme dilution is also thus avoided. The transfer of fluid is not merely a passive diffusion; the intestinal wall expends energy in active transport. Whether there is a further transit of fluid through the enveloping rectal wall is not known, but this would seem unlikely since the hind part of the mid-gut is directly continuous with the rectum.

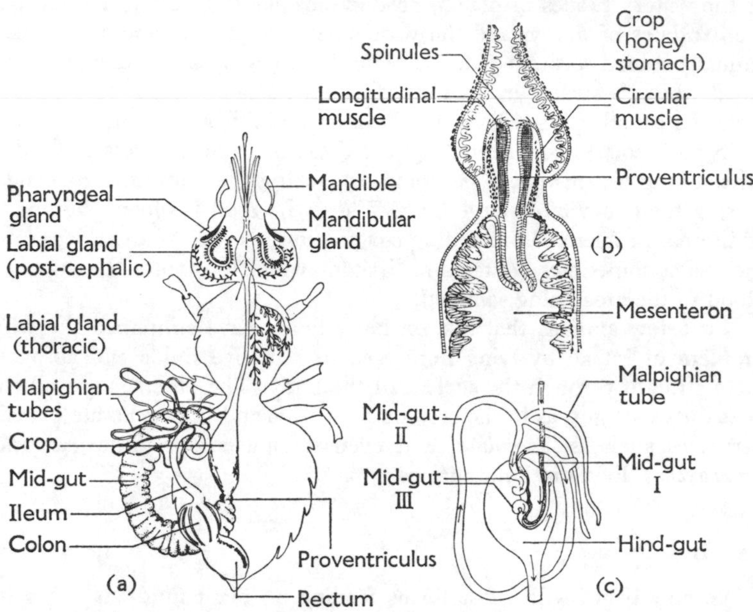

Fig. 6–1 **(a)** Alimentary canal of the honey bee, *Apis mellifica*. **(b)** Longitudinal section of the crop or honey stomach, proventriculus and mesenteron. **(c)** Alimentary canal of the coccid, *Lecanium*, showing the filter chamber formed of the first and last segments of the mid-gut.

The fluid excrement of coccids is very copious and contains much unabsorbed organic matter, especially sugars and other carbohydrates, furnishing the familiar honeydew coating the surfaces of leaves. The manna of biblical times seems to have been the honeydew of a coccid, *Trabutina mannipara*, living on tamarisk in Sinai. The vast excess of secreted sugar is surprising (manna contains 55 per cent sucrose, 25 per cent invert sugar and 19 per cent dextrin). Such large meals of sugary plant juice may perhaps serve to supply the insect's protein needs from the same sources, but this cannot be the whole truth since the excrement may contain up to 5 per cent of unused protein. Some other scarce nutritive substance is probably involved.

The need of accessory factors and trace substances may also explain the occurrence in most plant-sucking Hemiptera of specific micro-organisms carefully transmitted from one generation to another. In some insects the bacteria may live in pouches of the mid-gut, but in the coccids they are aggregated in 'mycetomes', strings of modified cells here contained within the fat-body. In blood-sucking insects bacteria occur too, but only in those taking a narrow diet of blood at all stages; sterile mammalian blood is an incomplete food and the bacteria are probably responsible for vitamin production.

The salivary glands and their secretions in the honey bee are complex and diverse (Fig. 6–1a and b). First there are the mandibular glands producing an acid secretion (pH 4.6–4.8); they are very active in the queen, less so in the workers and vestigial in the drones. Their secretion perhaps assists the softening of the cocoon at emergence. The second pair of glands, the pharyngeal glands, produce during the early life of the adult the royal jelly used in feeding the young stages of the queens. The bee requires pollen for these glands to become fully active, which happens 3–6 days after emergence. (The secretion has an acid reaction of pH 4.5–5.0.) When foraging begins at three weeks the glands switch over to the secretion of amylase and invertase, becoming most active at about a month, and being responsible for the presence of these enzymes in honey. The appearance of invertase at the onset of foraging is a good example of the phased production of enzymes in response to current metabolic needs. The third salivary glands, the labial glands, are in two divisions: posterior cephalic with a natural secretion of a fatty emulsion to work wax, and thoracic glands active throughout life, and producing no enzyme but a watery secretion (pH 6.3–7.0) probably used in comb-building.

Among the social Hymenoptera, the bees have developed a perfect apparatus for taking nectar which is converted to honey in the dilated crop known as the 'honey stomach' (Fig. 6–1b). No absorption takes place here and the exit to the mid-gut is guarded by the honey stopper, a special projection from the proventriculus. The lumen of the honey stopper is occluded by four converging, spinose lips. Pollen grains are seized by these and transferred without crushing into the mid-gut, leaving behind the fluid nectar. In a bee fed on a suspension of syrup with pollen grains the crop will remain tense with fluid while pollen is gradually removed. The grains are then separately digested, probably by enzymes reaching the pollen starch through the open micropyle. The waste from a meal is relatively small and may be long retained; in the young imago the huge distended rectum is not evacuated until foraging begins three weeks after hatching.

A number of insects are specialized for drawing off blood from living animals. The most important are the blood-sucking Hemiptera (such as *Cimex* and *Rhodnius*), the fleas (Siphonaptera) and the blood-sucking true flies or Diptera, including gnats, mosquitoes and the tsetse flies, *Glossina*. The last-named shows us a good example of the gut of a fluid-feeding dipteran (Fig. 6–2). The lancing and sucking mouth parts lack the stylets formed by the mandibles and maxillae in the mosquito; the labium forms a sharp chitinized probe and along it runs an injection needle, the hypopharynx, and a suction tube, the epipharynx. The saliva driven down the hypopharynx is not enzymic but contains an irritant and also keeps the mouth parts clean between feeding. It also provides in *Glossina* a powerful anticoagulin. If the salivary glands are removed the proboscis and crop become blocked with blood clots, but until this occurs feeding proceeds normally.

Blood passes straight to the crop, which in most Diptera is a diverticulum opening by a narrow duct and storing great amounts of fluid, to be released and passed on in similar instalments. In those mosquitoes that take sugary plant juices as well, these alone are stored in the crop, the blood meal being carried straight to the stomach.

In the adults and larvae of such Diptera as *Glossina* the peritrophic membrane is much more specialized in its formation than in the cockroach (p. 15). A single thin layer is secreted in viscous form by a ring of cells at

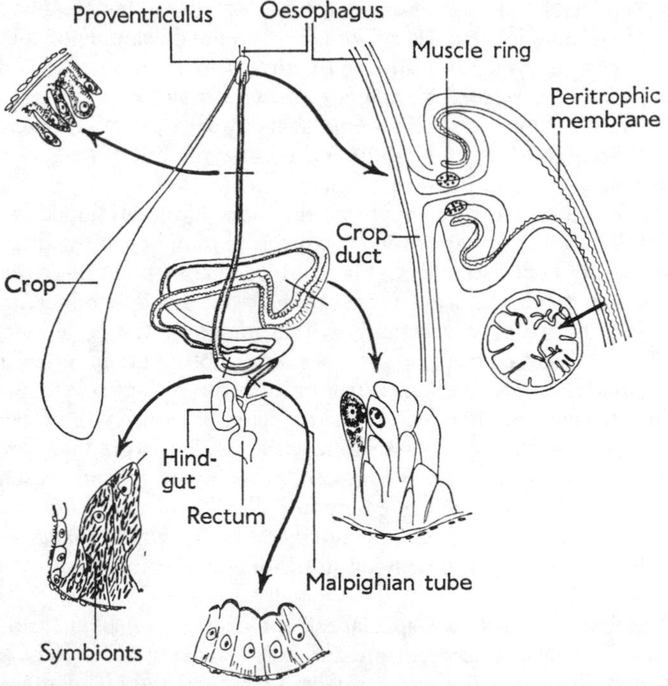

Fig. 6–2 Alimentary canal of tsetse fly, *Glossina*, with histological details of parts of the mid-gut and (right) enlarged view of the annular mould producing the peritrophic membrane. (Adapted from WIGGLESWORTH.)

the anterior limit of the mid-gut, and the secretion passes through a ring-shaped mould formed by an invagination of the oesophagus. Since the mid-gut is narrower than the mould that forms the membrane, the latter is thrown into deep longitudinal folds.

The mid-gut of *Glossina* shows great histological variation and division of labour. In the anterior segment the lining cells are pale-staining; the blood here becomes friable by the absorption of water, but no digestion occurs. Over a short length there is a zone of cells containing rod-like symbiotic bacteria. In the middle segment the cells are large and deep-staining, secreting enzymes, and the blood becomes blackened in contact with this epithelium. Carbohydrates are very feeble, but the proteases are highly active, being secreted under the stimulus of feeding; the medium is slightly acid (pH 6·5–6·6). The third segment, the narrow posterior part of the stomach, is lined with absorptive cells.

6.2 Mollusca

Among the Mollusca the small greenish or black sea-slugs of the opisthobranch order Sacoglossa are specialized for feeding on the cell contents of green algae. The radula is peculiarly fashioned, lying in a >-shaped tube, opening at its angle through the floor of the pharynx. Only one tooth is in use at a time, and these originate in the upper limb of the tube, the worn teeth detaching and passing into the lower limb. Sacoglossans are highly specific in their food plants, and the teeth which form tiny pointed blades are beautifully adapted to the cell size of the species concerned. Thus the British *Alderia modesta* sucks out the cell contents of *Vaucheria* with a filament diameter of 40–60 μ and its dental cusp is 33 to 35 μ long. The mode of feeding is very elegant: a kink of the filament is drawn between the lips of the mollusc and the cells lanced rapidly with a lengthwise incision; the colourless end of the filament is passed out, with its cells slit open and empty of green contents. The radula cusp is both a scalpel and a spoon, and as many as ten cells can be dealt with in a minute. The pharynx forms a powerful force pump, its roof being highly contractile, working in concert with an oesophageal valve near the entrance to the stomach. The stomach is merely a small annexe to the intestine, and provides openings to the long-branched digestive diverticula which enter the club-shaped outgrowths of the back, or cerata. The fluid gut contents flow freely in these, and impart their general colour to the animal. The chloroplasts of the alga are aggregated into spherules in the gut and can be seen to stream in and out of the diverticula by regular pulsations of the cerata.

The opisthobranchs are specialists in suctorial feeding although most of them feed on animal tissues. In *Onchidoris* and other slugs, for example, which suck out the cell contents of polyzoans, the buccal mass has developed a bulb-shaped pump. Dr. M. C. Miller has recently studied the feeding of a species of *Okenia* on the polyzoan *Zoobotryon* (Fig. 6–3c). The mouth fastens to the top of a zooecium, the radula works with rapid strokes and the buccal pump dilates to provide a suction force which draws the contents out of the horny zooecial wall. The polypide withdraws when the sucking is released, and the action is repeated several times, developing into a tug-of-war between the polypide and the slug. Once, however, the polypide has been sucked out of its house the mouth is closed and the subsequent pumping action of the bulb forces it along the oesophagus.

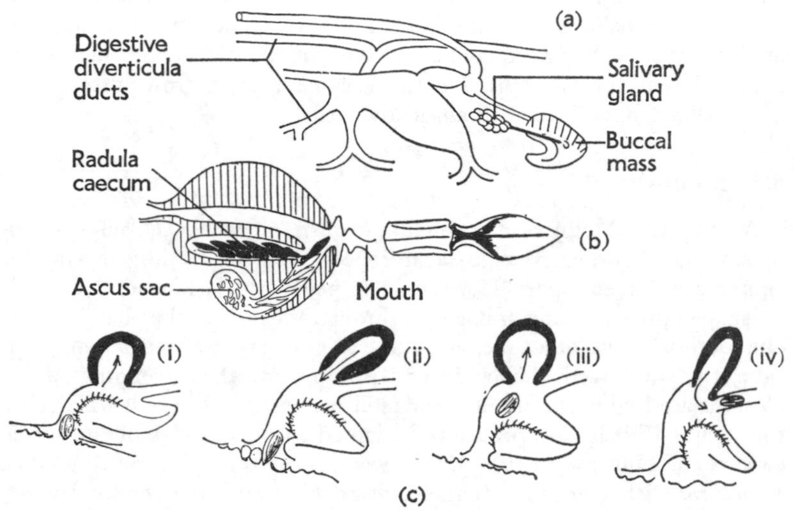

Fig. 6–3 (**a–c**) Suctorial opisthobranchs: (**a**) diagram of the gut of *Alderia modesta;* (**b**) sagittal section of the buccal mass of *Alderia* with a single, much enlarged tooth; (**c**) *Okenia plana*—stages in the action of the radula and buccal pump in removing a zooid from the polyzoan *Zoobotryon.* ((**a**) from EVANS.)

The aeolid nudibranchs feed upon coelenterates and have developed a wonderful adaptation for exploiting the stinging cells, or nematocysts, of the prey. These remain unexploded when the food is eaten and are arranged in the epithelium of the cnidosac, a small chamber which opens at the tip of each of the cerata, and communicates also with the ceratal branch of the digestive diverticulum. From this position the nematocysts can be shot out to the exterior when the aeolid is irritated.

6.3 Arachnida

All these arthropods, including spiders, scorpions, ticks and mites, are essentially suctorial feeders, even when they prey upon the whole bodies of larger animals. The spiders inject a strong salivary protease into the body of the prey, together with a disabling toxin contributed from the cheliceral glands. A captured fly is held close to the mouth by the pedipalps and the saliva is extruded drop by drop until the proteins are liquefied and digested, leaving the skin an empty husk within a few hours.

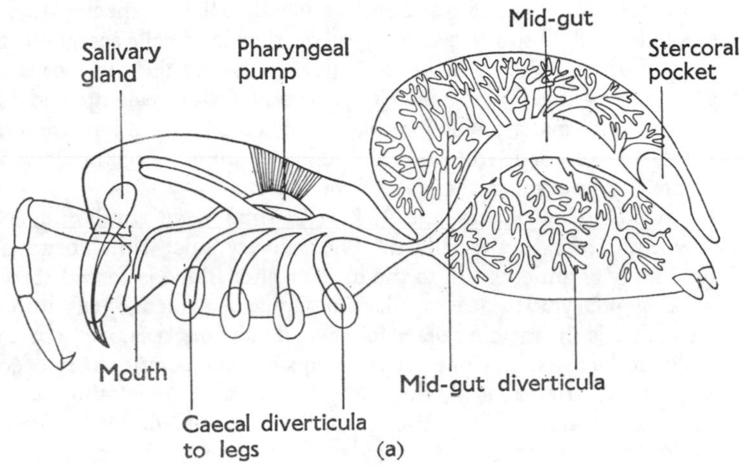

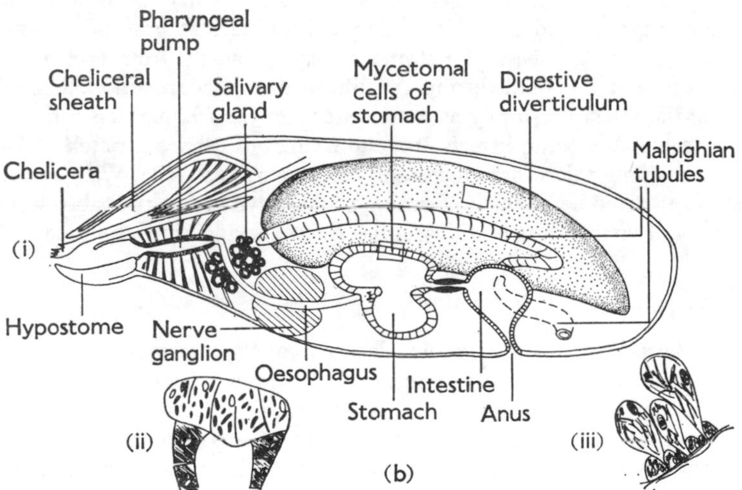

Fig. 6–4 **(a)** The digestive tract of a spider, showing the arrangement of the diverticula.
(b) The gut of the bird louse, *Ornithonyssus bacoti:* (i) whole animal in sagittal section, (ii) detail of mycetomal cells, and (iii) detail of pseudopodial digestive cells.

The narrow pharynx acts as a muscular pump to draw this fluid into the gut. The rest of the digestive tract provides all the room possible for great periodic intake of fluid. First, in the 'thorax' or prosoma, there are two large lateral caeca branching into the legs. Further back, in the 'abdomen' or opisthosoma, the diverticula are much finer and massed together in a soft, brownish grey, semifluid digestive gland. All this spacious system appears to be both absorptive and digestive: the gland cells secrete further enzymes into the ingested broth and other cells—or the same cells in a different phase—ingest and absorb. Senescent cells break up and form granules of faecal matter, which is sparse and voided only at long intervals; together with excretions from the Malpighian tubules, it accumulates in a plump stercoral pocket in the wall of the rectum.

The blood-sucking mites and ticks (Acarina) have similar ingestive arrangements, further specialized. The salivary duct runs forward to bring a supply of anticoagulin to the incision site. Blood is forced through the sucking pharynx into a capillary oesophagus which opens into the stomach. This is the meeting place for several pairs of caeca, very spacious, especially the lateral pair. Completely collapsible when empty, they become tensely inflated after a meal, the oesophageal valve preventing regurgitation from the stomach. As the stomach is distended, its lining cells stretch to a thin pavement and long glandular cells stretch far out into the lumen. These increase the digestive surface by penetrating into the blood mass, phagocytosing part-digested food. Their tips may be nipped off to liberate enzymes, and the effete cells yield up blackish granules of excrement. In the tick, *Ixodes*, the stomach may be cut off from the intestine and excrement is stored during the life in distended pseudopodial cells, leaving the intestine simply as a conduit from the Malpighian tubules.

As in blood-sucking insects, the stomach wall carries a patch of large cells containing micro-organisms and forming a mycetome. With a special diet of restricted content, the farming of these symbionts probably secures a supply of vitamins or other essential traces lacking from the food.

6.4 Leeches

The Hirudinea form a whole class of annelid worms given over to ectoparasitic blood sucking. The small freshwater *Glossiphonia*, feeding from molluscs such as *Lymnea* and *Planorbis*, gives us a representative picture of the parts of a leech's gut. The muscular proboscis receives at its base the ducts of numerous salivary glands. A narrow oesophagus leads back to a stomach with five pairs of spacious lateral caeca. The short intestine has four pairs of tiny diverticula, the lining of which forms a mycetome with symbiotic bacteria.

The course of digestion has been studied most in the medicinal leech *Hirudo*, which differs from *Glossiphonia* in having no proboscis but an armature of sharp jaws. The saliva contains a powerful anticoagulin.

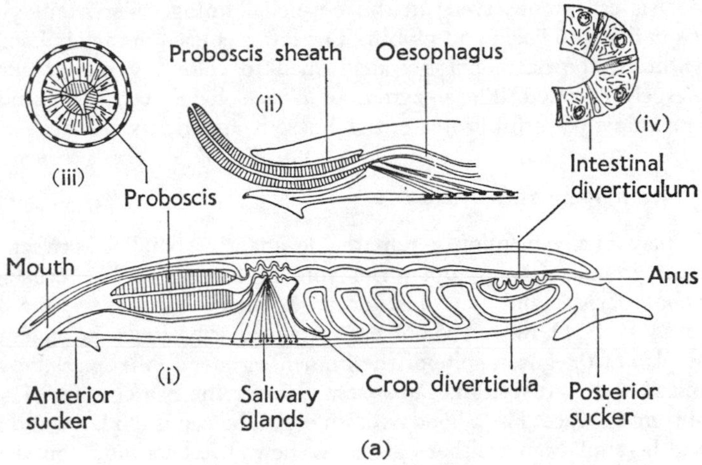

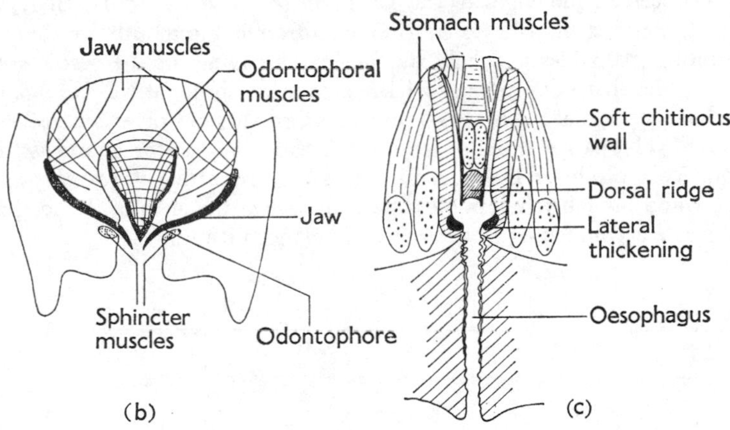

Fig. 6–5 (**a**) Gut of the freshwater leech, *Glossiphonia:* (i) whole animal in section, (iii) proboscis extended, with (ii) detail of proboscis in transverse section, and (iv) cells of intestinal diverticulum, containing symbionts. (**b**) Vertical section of the mouth and buccal mass of the opisthobranch mollusc, *Calma glaucoides.* (**c**) Comparable section through the mouth and fore-gut of the crustacean, *Nebaliopsis typica.* ((**b** & **c**) after ROWETT.)

Massive blood meals are stored in the caeca of the stomach which become distended to as much as ten times the leech's normal volume at a single meal. For days the blood undergoes no noticeable change—even its precipitins, antibodies and pathogenic bacteria can still be detected amidst a deposit of haemoglobin crystals. After weeks or months a process of haemolysis can be observed; in the epithelial lining cells, haemoglobin is broken down to haem and globin. The latter is used in metabolism and biosynthesis, the haem being transformed to colouring matter and its iron largely excreted. The enzymes of *Hirudo* have been little studied; they include a powerful protease, but lipase is apparently absent.

6.5 Two egg-suckers

We may finally mention a remarkable adaptive parallel between two different animals feeding upon the yolk of fish eggs. The crustacean *Nebaliopsis typica* and the opisthobranch *Calma glaucoïdes* have been shown by H. G. Q. Rowett to possess extraordinarily similar arrangements in the plan of the gut in spite of the immense general differences between a mollusc and a crustacean. *Calma* crawls over the egg clusters of shore fish, fitting its 'face' like a hood over an egg. The egg is too large and slippery to be swallowed, neither can it be chewed lest its fluid contents be washed away. It is thus held by folds of the lips and incised with three sharp processes, the edges of the jaws and the median radula. In *Nebaliopsis* the egg is thought to be pressed through the mouth by the soft non-biting mandibles and held by the 'crazy-paving' of the oesophageal cuticle. The sharp dorsal ridge of the stomach is brought to bear against the chitinous lateral thickenings, and cuts two slits out of which the yolk is sucked. This passes into the glandular digestive sac for storage and assimilation. Yolk produces little or no faeces; the intestine of *Nebaliopsis* is narrow and probably functionless, and in *Calma* the anus is closed, residual waste accumulating in the digestive gland during life.

Practical Work 7

The first and most engrossing laboratory work on the gut will be found in the study of its adaptive design. As the previous pages should have made clear, structure and function must be considered together—and more than any other of the major systems the gut lends itself to observation as a working system.

Useful laboratory material will be found in the various invertebrates in which the processes of the living gut can be watched in the intact animal. Best of all are probably the Crustacea. *Daphnia*, the water-flea, displays the full gut by transparency when immobilized in a cavity slide and its movements can be seen clearly. With slightly more difficulty the workings of the gastric mill of a prawn can be seen through the transparent carapace of the animal viewed under a binocular microscope. A cockroach with the wings removed and imprisoned in a wax chamber between two glass slides will—with sufficient transmitted light—show the movements of the various parts of the gut, particularly the action of the teeth in the proventriculus. The same observations can be made after removal of the dorsal body wall and placing the roach in insect perfusion fluid. Small transparent leeches such as *Glossiphonia* also make good material for the study of the live gut.

For observation of the rotating protostyle within the stomach there are two excellent sources of material. Living polyzoans, such as *Bugula* and *Membranipora*, can be viewed intact with the low power of the microscope showing the spinning of the pyloric rod, the movements of the stomach and the formation of faeces. Oyster spat, another good subject, should be collected fresh at the eyespot stage from between the gill lamellae of the parent *Ostrea edulis*. The rotations of the crystalline style can be readily observed and counted, as also the rhythmic contractile movements pumping material to and from the digestive diverticula. Feeding the spat with small green flagellates will allow observation of the course of digestion in the diverticula.

The use of indicators on the living gut demonstrates its range in pH values, with changes appropriate to control mucus viscosity or enzyme activity. Neutral red is a suitable wide range indicator which in dilute (0·02 per cent) solution can be employed to stain whole animals such as *Daphnia* or oyster spat. Below pH 6 it is red; rose at pH 7, orange at pH 8, yellow at pH 9. Better sensitivity may be obtained with several of the BDH indicators selected to cover different parts of the range. With larger animals gut fluids can be mixed with indicator for colour comparison in capillator tubes.

Methods for enzyme study can be applied to a wide variety of guts that can be assayed for digestive activity. Active extracts from small animals can be prepared by grinding pieces of gut in a little mortar made by roughening the bottom of a glass concavity with carborundum. Rinse with distilled water, making up to appropriate dilution and centrifuge. Add 1 c.c. of the clear supernatant to the same amount of the substrate in a small test-tube and incubate at, say, 25° for an hour or longer.

For amylase tests use a 1 per cent starch solution, measuring the progress of digestion by mixing a drop of substrate with a drop of iodine on a porcelain plate. Loss of blue colour indicates completion of digestion; or the whole sample can be made blue with iodine and the time of reaching end-point noted. Test on completion with Fehling's or Benedict's solution for the production of reducing sugar. Solutions of the crystalline style of molluscs should be tested for amylolytic action.

For invertase use a sucrose substrate, testing with Fehling's or Benedict's solution (for details see any elementary physiology manual). A good substrate for cellulase detection can be made by digesting high quality filter papers with concentrated sulphuric acid, repeatedly washing the white pulp so produced and making a pale suspension in distilled water of a little of the powdery precipitate. The course of digestion, with the removal of fine cellulose particles from the suspension, can be followed by measuring the decreasing optical density of the suspension with a photoelectric absorptiometer. Test finally or at known intervals with Fehling's or Benedict's solution for the production of reducing sugars.

Protein digestion can be studied most simply by incubating drops of the suspected gut extract upon the gelatin film of a developed photographic plate and noting after a given time the amount of erosion. Flakes of Congo-red-stained fibrin can be observed at intervals with the microscope. A better quantitative method, however, is to note the progressive digestion of small cubes of hard-boiled egg white, or of egg white in specially prepared 'Mett' tubes. These are made by filling 6 in. lengths of 1–2 mm glass tubing with strained egg albumen, sealing both ends in a flame and coagulating in boiling water. Cut into ½ in. lengths for use and record extent and rate of dissolution of the albumen column. Amino acid production may be tested for at end-point or at intervals by the standard procedure of formal titration.

Enzyme studies of the gut can be systematically carried out, region by region, and a chart drawn up showing the various enzymes present and their sites of greatest activity. The efficiency of the fluid gut contents should also be compared with that of contact digestion by the epithelial wall. Good results are obtained in this way with the mesenteric filaments of anemones. Cubes of liver or egg white may be offered to an intact anemone, and after a time interval extracted from the coelenteron to show their close investment by a coating of mesenteric filaments.

Experiments to ascertain the activity of enzymes with variation of temperature and of pH can easily be set up with the use of a simple water-bath or with pH controlled buffered solutions.

The saliva of medicinal leeches or of the land-leech, *Haemopus*, may be tested for the presence of an anticoagulin. Add a drop of salivary gland extract to a 1 c.c. sample of mammalian blood. Using as a control an extract of any other convenient invertebrate tissue, compare the times for coagulation in the two preparations. The thorax of a mosquito may be dissected for the salivary glands, or crushed and extracted, and a micro-test for for anticoagulin can be devised on similar lines. The mouth parts of the mosquito or of the bed-bug, *Cimex*, may be watched in action on the bare skin, and the inflation with blood of the crop diverticulum seen through the body wall. With the medicinal leech note the painless incision, the withdrawal of blood, and the triangular mark left by the jaws, as well as the continued flow of blood. Afterwards cleanse the site of incision carefully with antiseptic.

Histological preparations should be studied as widely as opportunity offers. The extent and thickness of the muscular wall should be noted in relation to the strength of peristalsis. The location and appearance of different types of epithelial cells, such as mucus-producing, ciliary and absorbing, may also be studied. In filter-feeding animals, the distribution of mucus can be beautifully revealed by several histological methods. Sections should be lightly stained in eosin, followed by the metachromatic stain thionine, giving various shades of mauve, purple, and black. Alternatively, after light haematoxylin or haemalum staining, mucus can be detected by its deep red reaction with mucicarmine.

Sites of absorption can be detected by the Prussian blue method, after feeding with materials containing powdered iron saccharate or other suitable iron compounds. Particles taken up by the cells can be demonstrated in situ by placing the sections, before staining, in potassium ferrocyanide to obtain a deep blue precipitate. Absorption of particles by amoebocytes can be well studied in sections from the stomach of suitably fed sea-urchins. Stomach contents can be carefully withdrawn from living mussels or oysters by inserting a cannula along the oesophagus at intervals after feeding. A useful experimental diet is that of nucleated red blood corpuscles of a fish in faint pink suspension in sea-water. Various stages of digestion of the haemoglobin and the nucleus can then be identified. In the oyster it should be possible to see the fed corpuscles engulfed by the bivalve's own amoebocytes, or lodged in the lining epithelial cells. Van Gieson's picrofuchsin is a useful stain to identify haemoglobin, in fixed sections, by the distinctive greenish colour imparted. In stomach contents of bivalves, spherules and waste droplets from the digestive gland can be identified in their various stages. Large and inert particles, easily identifiable, such as the diatom frustules in Kieselguhr (diatomaceous earth) may be administered to living bivalves; their distribution in sections reveals the areas of sorting and waste disposal.

Ciliary action can sometimes be watched in intact transparent guts. In larger animals the workings of the ciliary systems can be seen by carefully opening the living stomach and viewing with the binocular microscope under sea-water or perfusion fluid. Bivalves such as mussels or oysters are most likely to give good results. Small amounts of carmine-stained starch or carborundum powder may be pipetted on to the ciliated surfaces. The course of ciliary currents can sometimes be deduced from the fixed stomach by the shape and twisting of mucus strings, the location of rejected waste and the composition of faeces.

The most straightforward study of ciliary action can be made in the food-collecting ctenidia of a bivalve such as the sea-mussel, *Mytilus*. Ciliary sorting can also be observed on the inner faces of the labial palps of bivalves, where it closely resembles the same process in the interior of the stomach. The heaviest particles are rejected along grooves, the lightest kept afloat and eventually carried to the mouth. A preparation of the palp, carefully pinned out under sea-water can be presented with a mixture of recognizable particles of different sizes and weights, such as carmine, carborundum, diatomaceous earth, etc. Examining with the binocular, one can note the differences in the way such particles are disposed of; or, after allowing a bivalve to feed on such a mixture, differences may be looked for in the original composition and in that of the material pipetted from the stomach.

The symbiotic micro-organisms of various guts can often be clearly seen. Especially good collections of living flagellates are made by washing out with distilled water the rectum of termites and cellulose-feeding cockroaches. From the ruminant stomach, the ciliate protozoa need more careful precautions for study. If the laboratory is close to an abbatoir, or better still to a research station dealing with mammalian physiology, a vacuum flask of fresh rumen contents may be obtained, kept at blood temperature from the outset. Drops of this material, a greenish soup permeated with grass fragments, will show active *Entodinium* and other ciliates, but even a few minutes' drop in temperature will immobilize and kill them.

Whatever the variety of living material, the study of form and adaptation is still likely to be based in large part on the dissecting of preserved animals, the oldest and still the most instructive resource of the morphologist. Well-fixed material is always the most satisfactory to dissect first and generally gives the clearest morphological picture to the beginner. Thereafter all the various methods and techniques can be employed to examine the gut alive. Never neglect in dissecting to open the gut and view its interior thoroughly; the most valuable information lies within. Do not undervalue simple, straightforward methods of quick investigation: razor-cut whole sections of the whole fixed animal or its gut are among the most useful of all.

Fixation with Bouin's fluid is recommended for general purposes, followed by several days' washing and hardening in 80 per cent alcohol.

Further Reading

ANNISON, E. F. and LEWIS, D. (1959). *Metabolism in the Rumen*. Methuen, London.

BARRINGTON, E. J. W. (1941). *Phil. Trans. Roy. Soc. B*. **228**, 269. (Amphioxus)

BARRINGTON, E. J. W. (1962). Digestive Enzymes I. *Adv. Comp. Physiol. Biochem.*, **1**, 1–65.

*BELL, G. H., DAVIDSON, J. N. and SCARBOROUGH, H. (1963). *Textbook of Physiology and Biochemistry*, 5th edn. E. & S. Livingstone, Edinburgh. (Man)

BIDDER, A. M. (1950). *Quart. J. Micr. Sci.*, **91**, 1. (Cephalopoda)

FARNER, D. S. (1960). Chapter 11 in *Biology and Comparative Physiology of Birds*, vols. 1 and 2. Edited by A. J. MARSHALL. Academic Press, New York and London. (Birds)

*FRETTER, V. and GRAHAM, A. (1962). *British Prosobranch Molluscs*. Ray Society, London (Gastropoda)

GRAHAM, A. (1949). *Trans. roy. Soc. Edin.*, **61**, 737. (Molluscan stomach)

GRASSE, P. P., Ed. (1959). Annélides, in *Traité de Zoologie*, tome 5, fasc. 1. Masson et Cie., Paris (Leech)

HOWELLS, H. H. (1942). *Quart. J. micr. Sci.*, **83**, 357. (*Aplysia*)

HUGHES, T. E. (1959). *Mites, or the Acari*. Athlone Press, London. (Mites)

KERMACK, D. M. (1955). *Proc. zool. Soc. Lond.*, **125**, 347. (*Arenicola*)

MILLAR, R. H. (1953). *Ciona*. L.M.B.C. Memoir 25. Liverpool Univ. Press, Liverpool. (Ascidians)

*MORTON, J. E. (1960). *Biol. Rev.*, **35**, 92–140. (Ciliary feeders)

NICOL, J. A. C. (1959). *J. mar. biol. Ass. U.K.*, **38**, 469. (Anemone)

STOTT, F. C. (1955). *Proc. zool. Soc. Lond.*, **125**, 63. (*Echinus*)

*WIGGLESWORTH, V. B. (1929). *Principles of Insect Physiology*, 5th edn. Methuen, London.

YONGE, C. M. (1924). *J. exp. Biol.*, **1**, 343. (*Nephrops*)

YONGE, C. M. (1926). *J. mar. biol. Ass. U.K.*, **14**, 295. (*Ostrea*)

YONGE, C. M. (1937). *Biol. Rev.*, **12**, 87. (Metazoan digestive system)

* These works contain particularly useful bibliographies.